WORLD AT WAR

British tank, 1917.

WORLD AT WAR

ROBIN CROSS

This edition is published by
Mustard 1999
Mustard is an imprint of Parragon

Parragon
Queen Street House
4 Queen Street
Bath BA1 1HE, UK

Designed, produced and packaged
by Touchstone
Old Chapel Studio, Plain Road,
Marden, Tonbridge, Kent TN12 9LS, UK

Picture Research:
Brooks Krikler Research

Maps: HardLines

ISBN 1-84164-300-9

Printed in Italy

Above: Crash landing of F6F on USS Enterprise. Officer trying to rescue the pilot, November 1943.

Previous pages: St. Paul's Cathedral during the great fire raid, 29 December 1940.

Picture Credits:
(Abbreviations: t = top, r = right, l = left, b = below)
Hulton-Deutsch Collection: pages 8, 9, 10, 11, 12, 13b, 14, 15, 16, 20, 21, 23, 25r, 27, 29, 31, 32, 34-35t, 36, 38, 39, 40, 41, 42, 43, 44, 45, 48, 49, 51b, 52, 53, 54, 55, 56b, 58, 59, 60, 61, 62, 63, 64, 65, 66, 67t, 69b, 70, 74, 75, 76, 77, 80, 81, 82, 83, 85, 87, 89t, 90, 91, 92l, 94, 95, 96, 97, 103t, 104-105, 105t, 106, 107b, 108t, 109t, 110, 111b, 113t, 113r, 117b, 119, 124t, 126, 127, 129b, 130, 148, 149t, 152-153, 153t, 155b, 156, 157, 159, 160, 161b, 162, 163, 167b, 169t, 169r, 172, 173t, 175, 178t, 180b, 182, 183t, 188, 189, 191r.
Novosti Picture Library (London): pages 13t, 57r, 78, 79, 121b, 122, 123b, 136t, 137, 138, 139, 164, 165, 179b, 180-181, 181, 191t.
Solution Pictures: pages 17, 22, 24b, 24-25, 33t, 34l, 34-35b, 35r, 37b, 46, 47b, 56-57, 67b, 68, 69t, 89b, 93t, 102, 103b, 155t, 168-169.
Mary Evans Picture Library: pages 18l, 30.
E. T. Archive: pages 18-19, 25b, 26, 28, 33b, 47t, 71t, 72, 73, 84, 86, 88-89, 92-93, 105r, 107t, 108b, 109b, 111t, 112-113, 114, 115, 116, 117t, 117r, 118, 123t, 124b, 128-129, 129t, 136b, 140, 142t, 146, 147, 149b, 154, 158, 166, 167r, 170, 174, 184, 185, 186, 187b, 192.
Tom Donovan Military Pictures: pages 37t, 50-51, 51t, 98.
Cross Archive: page 71b.
Imperial War Museum: pages 120, 121t, 132, 133, 134, 135, 144, 145, 161t, 161l, 176, 177, 178b, 179t, 179l.
Jerry Goldie: pages 125, 141, 142b, 143r, 153b, 167t, 171, 173b, 187t.
Frank Spooner: pages 130-131, 143b, 183b, 190, 191b.
Kobal Collection: page 151b.
Crown Film Unit: page 150t; **Two Cities Films:** page 150b; **Gainsborough Films:** page 151b (all courtesy of Kobal Collection).

CONTENTS

WORLD WAR I *IN PHOTOGRAPHS* 6

WORLD WAR II *IN PHOTOGRAPHS* 100

WORLD WAR I 1914–1918
Neutral states throught the war
Central powers at the outbreak of war
Entente powers at the outbreak of the war
States which joined central powers
Frontlines November 1918
Maximum advance of the central powers
Frontlines August 1914
Neutral states which later joined the Entente
Russo–German border early 1915
NORWAY
SWEDEN
RUSSIA
NORTH SEA
DENMARK
GREAT BRITAIN
GERMAN EMPIRE
FRANCE
SWITZERLA
AUSTRIA HUNGARY
ROMANIA
SERBIA
BULGARIA
MONTE NEGRO
ALBANIA
GREECE
OTTOMAN EMPIRE
PERSIA
SPAIN
CORSICA
SARDINIA
SICILY
BLACK SEA
MEDITERRANEAN SEA
ALGERIA
LIBYA
EGYPT
ARABIA
St Petersburg
Dorport
Pskov
Moscow
Riga
Dvinsk
Tilsit
Vilna
Minsk
Voronezh
Copenhagen
Hamburg
Berlin
Tannenberg
Baranovichi
London
Amsterdam
Begorod
Gomel
Calais
Cologne
Warsaw
Pinsk
R. Volga
R. Rhine
Verdun
Metz
Paris
Munich
Prague
R. Dnieper
R. Donets
Millerova
R. Don
Vienna
Azov
Berne
Odessa
Budapest
Lyon
R. Danube
Kerch
Petrovsk
Milan
Venice
Trieste
Belgrade
Sebastopol
Tiflis
Baku
Madrid
Bucharest
Batumi
Lisbon
R. Tagus
Marseilles
Treblizond
Sofia
Erzipean
Constantinople
Rome
Ankara
Bitlis
Thessalonika
Gallipoli
Rawanduz
Kitri
Tekrit
Aleppo
Ramadi
Athens
Bagdad
Damascus
Jerusalem
Cairo
THE WESTERN FRONT
Amsterdam
NETHERLANDS
The Hague
Rotterdam
NORTH SEA
GREAT BRITAIN
Zeebrugge
London
Antwerp
Ostend
Dunkirk
R. Yser
Ypres
R. Rhine
Armentières
ENGLISH CHANNEL
Namur
R. Meuse
Messines
Mons
Mainz
Loos
Artois region
Ardennes region
Cambrai
R. Sambre
Arras
Picardy region
R. Somme
Charleroi
Sedan
Amiens
Stenay
Noyon
Mézières
Thionville
Craonne
Argonne region
Verdun
Metz
Lemberg
Compiègne
Soissons
Lorraine region
R. Seine
Reims
R. Oise
Château-Thierry
Montfaucon
St Mihiel
Nancy
R. Marne
Paris
Epinal
R. Seine
German advance 1914
Trench warfare line 1917
Farthest German advance 1918
Front line at Armistice
Belfort
SWITZERLAND

WORLD WAR I
IN PHOTOGRAPHS

Canadian troops surrounded by trench mortar bombs, 1917.

THE FIRST SHOTS

ON 28 JUNE 1914, the Archduke Franz Ferdinand of Austria, heir to the monarchy of the Habsburgs, visited the Bosnian town of Sarajevo to inspect Austrian troops there. Bosnia, and its sister province Herzegovina, were former Turkish possessions which had been annexed by Austria-Hungary in 1908. Many of its Serb inhabitants were bitterly resentful at not being allowed to join Serbia, their native state. One of them, a grammar school student named Gavrilo Princip, assassinated the Archduke and his wife as they rode through the streets of Sarajevo in an open car.

On 28 July, Austria-Hungary retaliated by declaring war on Serbia, a diplomatic rather than a military move as it would take several weeks for the Austrians to mobilise. The Russians then stepped in on the side of the Serbs, their fellow-Slavs. The Russians could not allow the Serbs to be humiliated, nor permit the Austrians and their German ally to dominate the Balkans and, by extension, Russia's access to the Mediterranean through the Dardanelles Straits. Russia mobilized on 29 July 1914.

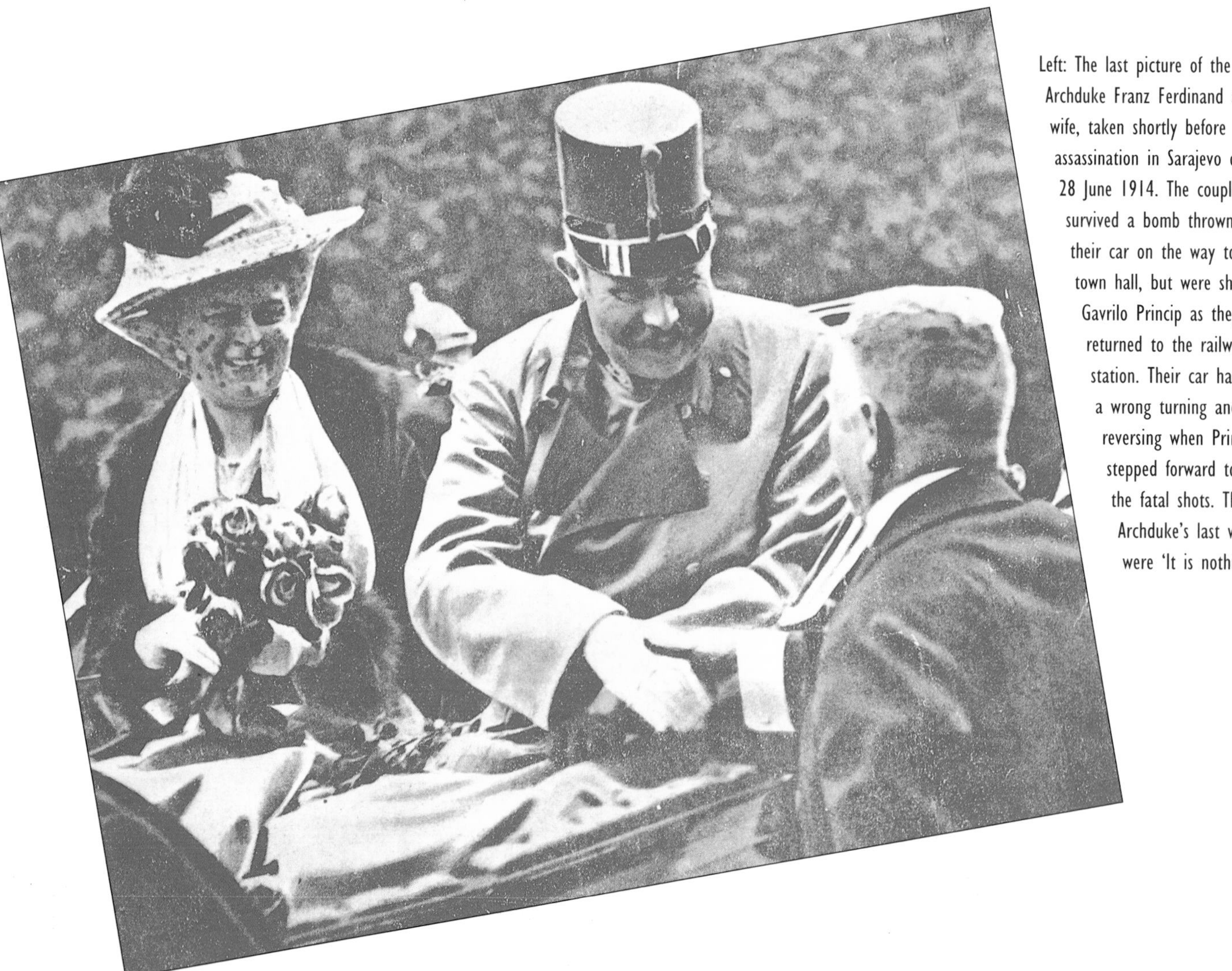

Left: The last picture of the Archduke Franz Ferdinand and his wife, taken shortly before his assassination in Sarajevo on 28 June 1914. The couple had survived a bomb thrown at their car on the way to the town hall, but were shot by Gavrilo Princip as they returned to the railway station. Their car had taken a wrong turning and was reversing when Princip stepped forward to fire the fatal shots. The Archduke's last words were 'It is nothing'.

On 1 August, Germany declared war on Russia and mobilised. Russia's ally France also mobilised on the same day. On 3 August, at 6.45pm, Germany declared war on France. The next day Germany invaded Belgium, which had been declared a neutral country by the Treaty of London in 1839. Now the British were drawn in. They sent Germany an ultimatum asking her to withdraw from Belgium. There was no reply and by midnight on 4 August, Britain and Germany were at war. The British had been the only nation to declare war on Germany rather than the other way round. As the British Foreign Secretary, Sir Edward Grey, waited for the midnight deadline, he remarked, *'The lamps are going out all over Europe. We shall not see them lit again in our time'.*

Left: Austria mobilizes. Men and boys cross Franz Josef Square in Vienna to join up. On 28 July Austria had declared war on Serbia. The German Kaiser Wilhelm II approved of the Austrian move, confident that Russia would not intervene. But the wheels of war were now in unstoppable motion.

Below: Before the storm. Warships of the Royal Navy visit the German naval base at Kiel while a Zeppelin hovers overhead. In 1912 Graf von Zeppelin's commercial airship company DELAG had been secretly informed that its crews were to join the military reserve and participate in regular exercises with the Army and the Navy.

WAR BY TIMETABLE

WHY DID Gavrilo Princip's shots in Sarajevo lead to a world war? At first the incident was hardly noted in Britain. Kaiser Wilhelm II of Germany did not believe that Russia would intervene on behalf of the Serbs. He was not going to let the crisis interfere with his planned holiday cruise. What went wrong?

Over the tangle of great power rivalry in Europe, with its shifting alliances and brutal jockeying for imperial position, lay the shadow of the huge conscript armies assembled by the continental powers in the late 19th century. Industrial muscle and expanding populations had produced deep pools of manpower which could be mobilized as acts of political policy to achieve national ends. The politicians calculated on their deterrent effect to avoid war, but did not anticipate that these great armies, accumulated to keep the peace, would once mobilized, propel the nations into war by their own fearful weight.

The staff of each army had prepared detailed war plans in advance. Those of Germany and France involved the use of precise railway timetables for the mass movement of men and material. The technological gears that made these movements possible could not be thrown into reverse by the politicians, who at this point had irrevocably surrendered control to their generals. In the first fortnight of August 1914, some 20 million men – nearly 10 per cent of the populations of the combatant states – donned uniforms and took the trains to war. All believed that they would be back home, *'before the leaves fell'*.

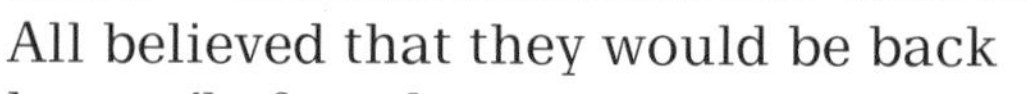

Left: General Sir Douglas Haig with Lord Haldane (right) in March 1914. Four months later Haig was on his way to France as commander of the British Expeditionary Force's I Corps. As Secretary of State for War, 1905-12, Haldane presided over a programme to modernize the British Army on European lines, creating a British Expeditionary Force (BEF) and a Territorial Reserve (TA) to provide reserves. Haldane's reforms ensured that the BEF crossed the Channel speedily and efficiently in August 1914.

Above: They thought it would be over by Christmas. Crowds in Trafalgar Square cheer Britain's declaration of war. Along the Mall and outside Buckingham Palace a throng of people sang 'God Save the King'.

Right: British volunteers undergo a medical examination at Marylebone grammar school in London. There were many rejects, the overall standard of health among working men being low, particularly in industrial areas. The youngster on the right looks well below the minimum age of 19.

THE BALANCE OF POWER

ON THE eve of war the German Army, drawing on a reserve of 4.3 million trained men, was organised in 25 army corps comprising 87 infantry and 11 cavalry divisions. The front-line army was supported by 32 highly capable reserve divisions. The German cavalry, diluted with light infantry to increase firepower, proved a disappointment in the opening phase of the war, as did the field artillery, with its standard equipment of the obsolescent 3-inch gun. The great strength of German artillery lay in its heavy guns for use in the field, particularly the 5.9-inch howitzer.

The polyglot army of Germany's Austro-Hungarian ally, with its 49 infantry divisions and 11 of cavalry, was more of a liability than an asset. Over 50 per cent of its troops were Slavs, Czechs and Italians – men whose natural sympathies lay with Austria's enemies rather than the Dual Monarchy. This was a factor behind some of the more spectacular Austrian collapses of the war. The fragility of the Austrian armies was exacerbated by the Chief of the Austrian General Staff, Field Marshal von Hötzendorf, whose strategic reach generally exceeded his grasp.

Above: Austrian troops bid farewell to their wives and sweethearts. The weakness of the polyglot Austro-Hungarian Army was revealed in its opening campaign of the war, when on 11 August it invaded Serbia. The Serbs threw the Austrians out and in turn invaded southern Hungary. It was the first of many Austrian defeats. The most reliable element in the Austro-Hungarian Army was its heavy artillery, the massive Skoda howitzers, which played an important part in German plans.

When mobilised, the Russians would field 114 infantry and 36 cavalry divisions, the legendary 'steamroller'. Although much had been done to revive it following the humiliating defeat by Japan in 1905, the Russian Army remained poorly equipped, with reserves of ammunition and rifles in short supply, desperately short of competent officers at the lower levels and riddled with corruption at the top

The French Army had made a remarkable recovery from the utter ruin of 1871 to field 75 infantry and 10 cavalry divisions infused with the doctrine of all-out attack developed after the disaster of the Franco-Prussian War. Symbolic of this spirit was the infantry's retention of conspicuous red trousers and heavy, dark blue coats. They were not replaced by 'horizon blue' uniforms until 1915.

Right: A newsreel camera catches Russian infantry on the way to the front in 1914. The Russian army was a clumsy giant, short of equipment and competent officers. But its illiterate peasant soldiery showed remarkable endurance throughout the war, supported by a tenacious artillery arm and the savage dash of the Cossack cavalry across the endless plains of eastern Europe.

From their small regular Army, the British supplied six infantry divisions and one and a half of cavalry for the Expeditionary Force to France. Compared with its European counterparts, the BEF was lavishly motorized, its 75,000 men supported by 1,485 motor vehicles of all kinds. The cavalry had useful mounted infantry training. The artillery's lack of heavy guns was balanced by the excellent 18-pounder field gun. However, the Army contained few officers with any experience of commanding large formations of men.

Below: Backbone of the French artillery, the quick-firing 75mm field gun introduced in 1897. By 1918 some 17,000 '75s' had been produced. Its hydro-pneumatic recoil system made the '75' very stable when fired and its quick-acting breech mechanism gave it a firing rate of up to 20 rounds a minute. It could throw a 12-pound high-explosive or 16-pound shrapnel shell up to 10,000 yards. However, French offensive doctrine meant that the '75' was not ideally suited to trench warfare, and the shells it fired were too light to pose a threat to heavily defended positions.

THE SCHLIEFFEN PLAN

IN THE 1890s the Chief of the German General Staff, Field Marshal Alfred von Schlieffen, turned his attention to Germany's fundamental strategic problem: how to cope with a war on two fronts; against Russia in the East and France in the West.

Schlieffen's solution was to seek a swift decision against France with the bulk of his forces while holding the Russians in check as they slowly mobilized. He intended to draw the bulk of the French Army towards the Rhine by leaving this sector weakly defended. The weight of the German blow was to be delivered in a swinging right hook through Belgium and northern France. Its extreme right would pass south of Paris, crossing the Seine near Rouen to take the French armies in the rear, pinning them against the Lorraine fortresses and the Swiss frontier.

Left: Alfred von Schlieffen (1833-1913), the German army's Chief of Staff, 1891-1906, who devised the plan to deal with war against Russia in the East and France in the West. France was to be overrun in the minimum time through the encirclement of her armies, making maximum use of railways, while a holding operation was mounted against the slowly mobilizing Russians in the East.

Right: In scorching summer heat, German infantry advance into Belgium in August 1914. The destruction of much of the railway system by the Belgian army meant that the critical distance between marching columns and railheads stretched to about 80 miles. Marching at a pace of 30 miles a day, the men of German First Army were reaching the point of exhaustion before the serious fighting had begun. There was no motor transport to help them. The five northern German armies operating between Luxembourg and Brussels had only 500 motor lorries between them.

After Schlieffen's retirement in 1906, the Plan was steadily watered down by his successor, von Moltke. The German left wing was strengthened at the expense of the all-important right. In August 1914 the Schlieffen Plan's ratio of forces between north and south had fallen from 7:1 to 3:1, depriving the right wing in the north of the strength to execute a complete encircling movement. Although the Plan had become unworkable, it was to exercise an inexorable influence on the inception and opening phase of the war.

Helmuth von Moltke, von Schlieffen's successor. He ignored von Schlieffen's dying words – 'Keep the right strong' – and fatally weakened the right wing of the German offensive against northern France, ensuring that it lacked the strength to accomplish a complete encirclement of the French armies. On 14 September 1914 he was replaced as Chief of Staff by General Erich von Falkenhayn.

THE BATTLE OF THE MARNE

THE OPENING days of August 1914 seemed to promise a fluid war of movement. While the Germans drove through Belgium, the French launched their own attack – Plan XVII – a headlong offensive in Alsace-Lorraine where German machine-guns mowed down thousands of men advancing in open order. However, as the German armies began to swing round into France, the Schlieffen Plan began to unravel. General von Kluck's First Army, on the extreme right, turned south-eastwards, exposing its flank as it marched obliquely across the face of the defences of Paris. Kluck was now passing east, rather than west of the French capital. This movement was reported by British aviators on 3 September.

The information made little impact on the slow-thinking French C-in-C, General Joffre, who was shuffling his forces to the left to protect Paris and to meet the Germans head-on. But its significance was not lost on General Galliéni, the military governor of Paris. On the morning of 4 September Galliéni ordered General Manoury's Sixth Army to prepare to strike at the German flank and rear. Engaged by Sixth Army on the 6th, Kluck turned west to meet the threat, simultaneously opening up a dangerous 30-mile gap between First Army and General von Bülow's Second Army, which was now taking the brunt of Joffre's counter-offensive.

The BEF, which had halted its retreat, now advanced cautiously into the gap with the French Fifth Army on its right. The nerve of the German C-in-C, von Moltke, far away in his HQ in Koblenz, cracked as he cast an anxious eye towards the Channel ports and the threat to his rear posed by the (unrealized) intervention of fresh British armies.

On 9 September he ordered Bülow and Kluck to retreat to the Noyon-Verdun line. The Allies tracked them for five days before being halted on the Aisne by a hastily improvized line of German trenches.

Right: The shape of things to come. British infantry entrenched near St Marguerite in September 1914. The BEF had already fought from trenches on the Mons-Conde canal during the Battle of Mons on 23 August, a rearguard action in the face of the advancing German First Army which played a part in unhinging the Schlieffen Plan.

Above: The spoils of war. French troops pose proudly with German equipment captured during the Battle of the Marne. The battle had been fought along a front of some 300 miles by a total of some two million men. French casualties were 250,000 and the Germans about 200,000, a portent of future slaughter.

Right: The casualties mount. British wounded arrive at Charing Cross Hospital in 1914. British losses during the first four months of the war shattered its small Regular Army, leaving only a framework for the new volunteer and conscript armies that were to come.

CHARING CROSS HOSPITAL
CHARING CROSS HOSPITAL
ENTRANCE
FOR
PATIENTS

THE RACE TO THE SEA

AFTER THE Battle of the Marne, both sides extended operations northwards, each trying to work round the other's flank. As this series of leapfrogging manoeuvres reached its conclusion, the BEF sought to deny the Channel ports to the Germans, crashing head-on into the Germans at Ypres on 20 October.

Such was the initial confusion among the British high command that the C-in-C, Sir John French, believed for at least 48 hours that he was attacking while his heavily outnumbered forces were barely holding their ground. His optimism gave way to something close to panic when he finally grasped the true nature of the BEF's position.

The British line held, supported by the French on their right. On the British left the Belgians opened sluice gates to halt the German advance. Bitter fighting on a narrow front continued until 11 November when torrential rain and snow halted the final German offensive. The First Battle of Ypres was the last chapter in the history of the old British Regular Army, of which nearly 80 per cent had been lost in the fighting. From the Channel to the Swiss frontier, both sides now began to dig in. Trench warfare had arrived.

Field Marshal Sir John French (1852-1925), commander of the BEF from August 1914 to December 1915. A peppery veteran of the Boer War, and a noted womanizer, French showed excellent fighting qualities in the opening battles of the war, but failed to establish a good working relationship with his French allies. The scale of British losses in 1915, notably at Ypres and Loos, led to French's replacement by General Sir Douglas Haig.

Right: German troops march through the streets of Brussels on 20 August 1914. British and French withdrawals during the opening encounters meant that henceforth the war would be fought on French soil, nothwithstanding the qualified victory gained by the Allies in the Battle of the Marne.

Below: Figures in a landscape. British infantry cross a Belgian field in October 1914 as the BEF advanced towards Ypres. The Battle of Ypres was almost the last occasion on the Western Front when horsed cavalry was able to perform its traditional role of reconnaissance.

MELIOR
MELIOR
JULES BLATON
CIGARE

TANNENBERG

IN A MILITARY convention with France, signed in 1913, the Russian Chief of the General Staff, General Jilinsky, pledged to put 800,000 men in the field by the 15th day of mobilization. On the outbreak of war, two Russian armies advanced into East Prussia, a tongue of land projecting across the River Niemen to the heart of Russia, flanked on the north by the Baltic Sea and the south by Russian Poland. Jilinsky's plan was for First Army, commanded by General Pavel Rennenkampf, to advance against the eastern tip of East Prussia while to his south, Second Army, led by General Alexander Samsonov, took the Germans in the rear, cutting off their line of retreat to the River Vistula.

The general commanding the German Eighth Army in East Prussia, von Prittwitz, panicked. He was immediately replaced by General Erich von Ludendorff who, lacking the rank to hold supreme command, acted as Chief of Staff to a nominal superior, General Paul von Hindenburg, brought out of retirement and squeezed into a uniform now too tight for him.

Even before Hindenburg and Ludendorff had arrived in East Prussia, the situation had been stabilized by one of Prittwitz's staff, Colonel Max Hoffmann. He had exploited the

Below: Cossack cavalry cut a dash for the camera. In August 1914 the Russian Army fielded 36 cavalry divisions. On the Eastern Front, which was never wholly deadlocked by trench warfare, cavalry had some freedom of manoeuvre. Over 4,000 cavalry charges were mounted on the Eastern Front, including the shattering of the Austro-Hungarian Seventh Army by Russian cavalry at Gorodenko in April 1915.

gap between the two Russian armies, separated by the Masurian Lakes, to mount a delaying action in the north while concentrating in the south against Samsonov, whose sluggish advance was spread over a front of 60 miles. Ludendorff finished the job by enveloping Second Army and taking 125,000 prisoners. The unknown number of dead included Samsonov, who committed suicide on 28 August. The Germans then turned on First Army, which fell back in disorder after suffering a crushing defeat at the Battle of the Masurian Lakes. German casualties in the two battles were fewer than 25,000 men.

Left: The victors of Tanneberg, Ludendorff (left), Hindenburg (centre) and Hoffmann (right). Their task was made easier by the Russian habit of sending their wireless messages en clair, code apparently being too difficult for them.

Below: Huddled masses. Captured Russian troops of Second Army after the Battle of Tannenberg. The German victory at Tannenberg ensured that German territory remained clear of Russian troops for the duration of the war.

THE TRENCHES 1

THE OPENING weeks of fighting had given the false impression of a war of movement. But in September 1914, as each side tried to outflank the other in the 'Race to the Sea', the first trenches – initially mere scrapes in the ground – began to make their appearance. Within weeks the stalemate they had produced on the Aisne spread down the 500-mile battle line from the North Sea to the Swiss frontier.

At first the picture they presented on the long, congealed front was by no means uniform. The Germans packed troops into the front line with little immediate support beyond some machine-gun positions. In contrast, the British, in the low-lying, frequently flooded coastal plain of the Yser, quickly dug a three-line system of front, support and reserve trenches linked by zig-zag communications trenches.

The British system set the basic pattern which troops endured for the next four years, from Flanders to the dry chalklands of the Somme and Champagne to the wooded terrain of the Vosges. Beyond the trenches, at a grenade throw's distance, lay the barbed wire entanglements, and beyond that the narrow strip which divided the opposing trenches – 'no man's land'. Its width varied from sector to sector, from as much as 500 yards to as little as 50. Near Zonnebecke in 1915 the British and Germans were only 10 yards apart.

Right: Men of the 42nd East Lancashire Division in a sap-head at Givenchy in January 1918. These positions, about 30 yards forward of the front-line trenches, were listening posts where at night sentries would strain to detect signs of enemy movement. The sap-heads were often built in shell craters. From 1916 a shell falling in no man's land would spark a series of bloody little battles as each side tried to seize the new crater and connect it to their own lines with a sap trench. Note the camouflaged persicope in the middle of the parapet.

Below: Men of the Royal Scots Fusiliers muffled againt the winter damp at La Boutillière in 1914. The white goatskin worn by the man in the foreground was an especially prized item. In wet weather the men's greatcoats could absorb an extra 35 pounds of water and caked mud. Added to 60 pounds of equipment, this turned the simple business of moving about into an ordeal.

Right: British troops share a trench with French infantry. The wattle revettements in the left foreground indicate that this is a French trench. The French avoided packing their front line, and thus leaving insufficient reserves to counter a breakthrough, by dividing the front line into what they termed 'active' and 'passive' zones. The former were strongly fortified and gave flanking fire to the passive zones on either side. The latter were heavily wired but lightly manned. Behind the front line was a network of shell-proof strongpoints and then a 'stop line' two miles to the rear, again divided into active and passive zones.

THE TRENCHES 2

AS THE war progressed, trench engineering became ever more elaborate. The German Hindenburg Line, built in the winter of 1916-17, consisted of three lines of double trenches to a depth of two miles, the first of which was protected by six belts of barbed wire, the densest of them 100 yards thick. Dozens of communications trenches linked the lines and to the rear were sited hundreds of guns zeroed to plaster 'no man's land' with shrapnel and high explosive or gas shells. Further forward, machine guns with interlocking fields of fire were positioned to strafe 'no man's land' the moment the enemy went 'over the top'. Railways were built right up to the rear areas to speed reinforcement and supply.

Living conditions in the trenches were often grim. During the wet season, they became morasses, particularly in the British sector on the Western Front. Men and mules could drown in the glutinous mud. Wounded men were particularly vulnerable. A survivor of Passchendaele recalled finding: *'A khaki-clad leg, three heads in a row, the rest of the bodies submerged, giving one the idea that they had used their last ounce of strength to keep their heads above the rising water. In another miniature pond, a hand still gripping a rifle is all that is visible while its next door neighbour is occupied by a steel helmet and half a head, the eyes staring icily at the green slime which floats on the surface almost at their level.'*

Above: Men of British 8th Division snatch exhausted sleep in a captured German trench at Ovillers during the Battle of the Somme in July 1916. A comrade keeps watch on the parados, the back wall of the trench. Note the firestep on the left, used by those on sentry duty or an entire unit when standing to face an enemy attack.

Left: On the Western Front two of the British soldier's greatest enemies were water and mud, the latter making even the shortest journey a nightmare. In July 1916 a Guards battalion lost 16 men through exhaustion and drowning in the mud. When an officer was ordered to consolidate his position, he replied, 'It is impossible to consolidate porridge'.

Above: German soldiers take time off in their dug-outs to examine their clothes for the eggs of lice, another scourge of the trenches, which caused frenzied scratching and carried a disease known as 'trench fever'. In 1917 it accounted for 15 per cent of all cases of sickness in the British Army. One British officer noted that 'captured German trenches on the Western Front sometimes had a species of small red lice crawling over their walls and blankets'.

Left: A pack horse loaded with trench boots struggles through the mud near Beaumont-Hamel in November 1916. Each British division was issued with about 2,500 pairs of these thigh-length gumboots. The Germans supplied thousands of waterproof overalls for men in the front line. A French officer wrote of these conditions: 'These days a sea of mud. The badly wounded are drowned as they try to drag themselves to the aid post. . . Dirty cartridges, rifles whose clogged mechanisms won't work any more; the men pissed in them to make them fire'.

THE TRENCHES 3

SANITARY CONDITIONS in the trenches were appalling. Rats gorged themselves on corpses lying in 'no man's land' or embedded in the walls of the trenches themselves. Trench foot and frostbite claimed about 75,000 British casualties during the war. On 'quiet' sectors boredom was a deadly enemy, although even here artillery, snipers and mortars caused a steady stream of casualties. During two months in the Neuve Chapelle sector in late 1916, the 13th Yorkshire and Lancashire lost 255 men although they had been on the defensive the whole time.

The tedium of trench routine was broken by the German dawn barrage and the Allies' reply at sunset, each side using the glare of the sun behind them to prevent the enemy from registering the position of their batteries. At night, patrols and trench raiding parties moved through the lunar landscape of 'no man's land'; wiring parties, burial details and re-supply detachments went warily about their business, keeping an eye open for star shell or enemy patrols, while the latest batch of wounded went 'down the line' to the rear.

Right: British troops savour the intimate fug of a rear-area dug-out, many of which were built in converted cellars in ruined towns and villages. Dug-outs varied hugely in size, comfort and security, from the scraped-out individual 'funk-holes' in the sides of front-line trenches to the often lavish accommodation provided in the German rear, which was provided with electric light, ventilation and solidly planked floors. Rear-area dug-outs were the deepest; the heavy artillery on both sides rarely bombarded front-line trenches for fear of dropping a near-miss on their own lines or undermining their own trenches.

Below: A German dug-out and its former occupant. An added danger of the trenches was posed by mines. Engineers on both sides dug tunnels under the enemy's lines in which huge mines were exploded just before an attack. When the British detonated 19 gigantic mines on the Messines Ridge on 7 June 1917, the sound of the explosions could be heard in London.

The British maintained morale with regular rotation between front, support and reserve positions, the arrival of letters and parcels from home and a concerted programme of recreational activities. However, experience in the front line was typically summed up in the soldiers' dirge:

'The world wasn't made in a day
And Eve didn't ride on a bus
But most of the world's in a sandbag
And the rest of it's plastered on us!'

Above: The battlefield at night. Shell fire, tracer flares and signal rockets frequently lit up the lunar landscape of 'no man's land' as trench raiding parties went about their business.

GAS

Right: German stormtroopers burst through a cloud of phosgene gas, which had been developed in 1915. The poet Wilfred Owen, who fought with the Manchester Regiment, wrote of a man exposed to phosgene gas:

'. . .the white eyes writhing in his face,
his hanging face, like a devil's sick of sin;
If you could hear, at every holt, the blood
Come gargling from the froth-corrupted lungs,
Obscene as cancer, bitter as the cud
Of vile, incurable sores on innocent tongues."

AT 5pm ON 22 APRIL 1915 two sinister greenish-yellow clouds crept across 'no-man's-land' towards the Allied lines at Ypres. They were pressurized chlorine gas released from over 500 cylinders in the German trenches as the preliminary to a major offensive. German prisoners and a deserter had warned of this new tactic, but no countermeasures had been taken. The two French colonial divisions on the north flank of the Ypres salient were engulfed by the cloud and fled in panic, leaving a four-mile gap in the front peopled only by the dead and those who lay suffocating in agony from chlorine gas poisoning. Having achieved total surprise, the Germans failed to exploit the breakthrough. Nevertheless, the gas had caused at least 15,000 casualties, 5,000 of them fatal.

Chlorine gas poisoning led to a slow and agonizing death by asphyxiation. On 25 September 1915 the British released chlorine gas on the German lines at Loos but little of it reached the enemy trenches. Thereafter increasing use was made of gas shells. Some 63 types of gas had been developed by 1918 but the most familiar was mustard gas, smelling like a *'rich bon-bon filled with perfumed soap'*, which literally rotted the body within and without.

The first countermeasures against gas were primitive, among them pads of cotton waste soaked in urine. The chlorine gas was partially neutralized by the ammonia in the urine. The famous box respirator did not appear until the winter of 1917 and soon became standard issue for troops at the front. Gas caused nearly a million casualties during the war, although this is only a conservative estimate.

Above: British machine-gunners protected against gas at Ovillers during the Battle of the Somme, July 1916. They are wearing grey flannel hoods with mica eye-pieces impregnated with phenol. A rubber-tipped metal tube was clenched between the teeth for exhalation.

Right: A German anti-aircraft crew in box respirator gas masks.

1915 – YEAR OF THE BIG PUSH

IN THE opening campaign of the war the Germans had occupied much of Belgium and tracts of the industrial region of northern France. This enabled them to assume a defensive posture in the West while pursuing territorial ambitions in the East. The British and French had no such luxury. For them, the winning back of the territory lost in 1914 was a strategic necessity.

The British launched their first attempt to break the German line at Neuve Chapelle in March 1915. The battle saw a number of innovations: the extensive aerial photo-reconnaissance of the German positions; the co-ordination of artillery fire by timetable to fit the projected lines of advance; and the laying of an experimental network of field telephones before the attack went in. After a short 'hurricane' bombardment the British attacked on a narrow front with a numerical advantage of 35:1. They achieved an initial breakthrough before communications broke down, ammunition ran out and the advance stuttered to a halt – the pattern for future battles on the Western Front.

The British lost 13,000 men at Neuve Chapelle. In September, amid the slagheaps and ruined mining towns of Loos, they lost another 65,000 supporting a major French offensive in Champagne which suffered 190,000 casualties. There had been no strategic gain, only slaughter. In Britain, the shortage of shells caused a public outcry which led to the establishment of a Ministry of Munitions under David Lloyd George.

Below: A propaganda poster paints a heroic picture of Neuve Chapelle, but the casualty figures for the early summer of 1915 make grim reading. At the Battle of Aubers Ridge in May, 15 German companies and 22 machine-guns broke up an attack by three full British brigades. In an attack by the 1st Battalion of the Black Watch, only 50 men reached the German trenches alive. In the first two hours of the Battle of Loos, the 15th Division lost 60 per cent of its men. When 12 fresh battalions attacked on the second day – a total of 10,000 men – they sustained nearly 8,300 casualties. German machine-gunners watched as the British fell 'literally in hundreds'.

Above: Fraternization between French and British troops. Their sacrifice in 1915 had been in vain, but the French C-in-C, Joffre, remained confident that he was wearing the Germans down. However, the Franco-British offensives did little to distract the Germans from their business on the Eastern Front and the Balkans, where Serbia had been knocked out of the war.

Right: David Lloyd George, Minister of Munitions, and Winston Churchill, First Lord of the Admiralty, in Whitehall, October 1915. Both men were 'Easterners', wedded to the strategy of defeating Germany by an 'indirect approach' against her allies. In contrast, the soldiers to whom the politicians had ceded the overall conduct of the war believed that Germany could be overcome only on the Western Front, where her armies were the strongest. Lloyd George, who had originally opposed the war, had been appointed Minister of Munitions in June 1915, became War Secretary in June 1916, following the death of Kitchener, and Prime Minister the following December.

THE WAR OF THE GUNS

WITH THE arrival of fixed trench systems the war on the Western Front took on many of the aspects of a gigantic siege, requiring colossal quantities of all types of guns and projectiles. In August 1914 the first six divisions of the BEF fielded 486 guns, all but one of them light field pieces. By November 1918 the number of British guns in France had risen to 6,432 of all types.

During the war the British artillery loosed off over 170 million rounds, representing more than five million tons. During the two weeks preceding the Passchendaele offensive, in July 1917, British guns fired 4,283,550 rounds at a cost of some 22 million pounds sterling. At Messines in June 1917, the British concentrated 2,338 guns (808 of them heavy) and 304 large smooth-bore trench mortars on a nine-mile front, a ratio of one gun to every seven yards or 240 to the mile. In the 17-day preliminary bombardment, 5.5 tons of ammunition were delivered to each yard of enemy front.

Artillery accounted for up to 70 per cent of the casualties between 1914 and 1918. Troops subjected to heavy bombardment endured physical and mental torture. A French infantry sergeant likened the ordeal to being *'tied to a post and threatened by a fellow swinging a sledgehammer. Now the hammer is swung back for blow, now it whirls forward, till, just missing your skull, it sends the splinters flying from the post once more. This is exactly what it feels like to be under heavy shelling'.* Nevertheless, even after the heaviest bombardment sufficient soldiers survived to break up an infantry attack. The 4.3 million shells fired in the 14 days before the offensive at Passchendaele failed to suppress the defence. When the British went over the top, the German machine guns were waiting for them.

Below: An American heavy battery in action. The effect of persistent barrages was psychologically shattering. One British officer observed, 'Modern warfare reduces men to shivering beasts. There isn't a man who can stand shell-fire of the modern kind without getting the blues.' Another recalled that 'a barrage hung over us. It seemed as though the air was full of vast and agonized passion, bursting now with groans and sighs, now into shrill screaming. . . shuddering beneath terrible blows'.

Left: The sinews of war. Howitzer barrels swing over the shop floor at a war factory in Coventry.

Below: A British 60-pounder in action, March 1918, during the second Battle of the Somme. The 60-pounder also saw sterling service in Mesopotamia. Until the last months of the war on the Western Front, heavy bombardment often failed to destroy the enemy barbed wire, and by breaking up the ground created a new obstacle. In the Flanders plain, where the water table was high and the drainage system close to the surface, the results were disastrous.

THE DARDANELLES

IN OCTOBER 1914 Turkey entered the war on the side of the Central Powers. In Britain, operations against the Turks were considered necessary both to safeguard the Suez Canal and to relieve the pressure on the Russians by opening up a supply and communications route to them through the Dardanelles Straits, the passage from the Aegean to the Black Sea. A lodgement on the Gallipoli peninsula, on the northern side of the Straits, would also provide a springboard for a drive to Istanbul, forcing the Germans to withdraw troops from the Western Front. This was the argument advanced by the so-called 'Easterners', notably Winston Churchill, First Lord of the Admiralty.

A Franco-British naval attempt to force the Dardanelles in March 1915 came to grief on Turkish minefields. A hastily assembled expeditionary force of 80,000 men, commanded by General Sir Ian Hamilton, landed on the rocky coastline of the Gallipoli peninsula on 25 April. The Turks were taken by surprise, but Hamilton's timid generalship allowed them to rush up reinforcements and trap his men in their landing areas. The British element in the expeditionary force and the Australian and New Zealand Army Corps (ANZAC) were to be pinned down for almost a year. Trench warfare ensued, in conditions far worse than those in France. The British and Anzacs held no secure rear, only beaches exposed to Turkish shellfire. Everything – even water – had to be landed at night. Disease, particularly dysentery, took a terrible toll.

Above: The combined British and French fleet attempts to force the Dardanelles on 19 February 1915. The operation was suspended when on 18 March three capital ships were sunk and a fourth damaged by a combination of mines and shore-battery fire. World War I was the last conflict in which the battleship would be regarded as the main instrument of naval power.

Above: Turkish shells burst near the grounded *SS River Clyde* on 'V' beach at Gallipoli, 25 April 1915. The *River Clyde*, an old collier, had been converted into a crude infantry landing ship, with doors cut in her sides, but she grounded in water too deep for the men to wade ashore. Many drowned under the weight of their equipment. Under murderous Turkish fire, the sea ran red with blood up to 50 yards from the shore.

Two more landings at the beginning of August, offered a fleeting chance of a breakout from the beachheads, but the chance was frittered away. The troops were evacuated in December without a man being lost. The Dardanelles fiasco led to Churchill's resignation and the end of the Liberal government in Britain.

Above: Anzacs in action. At 'Lone Pine Ridge' in August 1915, seven Victoria Crosses, Britain's higest award for gallantry, were won. At Gallipoli the British French and Anzac forces deployed finally numbered some 489,000. British casualties were 213,980, of which at least 145,000 were due to sickness. Turkish losses were as high as 350,000.

Below: A precarious bivouac for a British cavalry regiment. The stalemate of the Western Front was reproduced at Gallipoli, accompanied by the miseries of dysentery and enteric fever. The freezing weather in November 1915 produced 15,000 cases of frostbite.

THE WAR AT SEA

WHEN WAR broke out, Admiral Beatty, commander of the Royal Navy's battlecruiser squadron, exulted, *'For thirty years I've waited for this day!'* The German High Seas Fleet did not oblige the flamboyant Beatty. Most of it withdrew to port. The losses the Germans sustained in the action off the Heligoland Bight on 28 August, when Beatty's battlecruisers sank three light cruisers and a destroyer, reinforced the German high command's reluctance to risk its battle fleet in the North Sea.

The German navy hit back on 1 November off the coast of Chile, where its China Squadron, commanded by Admiral Graf von Spee, destroyed a squadron of obsolescent British cruisers. Spee's success was short-lived. His two battlecruisers, *Scharnhorst* and *Gneisenau*, were hunted down and sunk off the Falkland Islands by a British task force led by the battlecruisers *Invincible* and *Inflexible*.

Meanwhile, the Germans continued to play tip and run in the North Sea. On 16 December their battlecruisers bombarded the coastal towns of Scarborough, Hartlepool and Whitby. Five weeks later, on 24 January 1915, on another sweep into the North Sea, a German force of three battlecruisers, five cruisers and 22 destroyers, commanded by Vice-Admiral von Hipper, was intercepted by Beatty's battlecruiser squadron. In the ensuing Battle of Dogger Bank the British sank the elderly cruiser *Blücher* and badly mauled the rest of Hipper's force before he slipped away.

Admiral Sir David Beatty (1871-1936), commander of the Royal Navy's battlecruiser squadron, 1913-17. Beatty led the action at Heliogoland in August 1914 and played an important part in the Battle of Jutland in 1916. He was appointed Commander of the Grand Fleet in 1917 and served as First Sea Lord, 1919-27.

Left: Britain's Grand Fleet, steaming in line ahead at the Battle of Jutland, May 1916. In the summer of 1914 it counted 20 dreadnought battleships on its strength, nine 'dreadnought-type' battlecruisers and 41 pre-dreadnoughts; 12 dreadnoughts and one battlecruiser were being built. In comparison, the German High Seas Fleet had only 13 dreadnoughts, five battlecruisers and 22 pre-dreadnoughts with seven dreadnoughts and three cruisers building. Thus the potential capital ship ratio was 42:28 in favour of the Grand Fleet.

Below: German survivors are picked up by the British battlecruisers *Inflexible* and *Invincible* after the Battle of the Falkland Islands, December 1914.

JUTLAND – CLASH OF THE DREADNOUGHTS

CONFRONTED with the numerically superior Royal Navy, Vice-Admiral Scheer, who had assumed command of the German High Seas Fleet, hoped to entice elements of the British Grand Fleet into a series of isolated actions in which the latter's strength would be worn down. However, the Royal Navy was able to anticipate the moves in this strategy thanks to the capture, early in the war, of the Germans' signals and cipher books.

On 30 May 1916, Admiral Sir John Jellicoe, commander of the Grand Fleet, learned via intercepted radio messages that the German fleet was sailing from Wilhelmshaven. In the vanguard was Vice-Admiral von Hipper's Scouting Force of battlecruisers and light cruisers, the bait to lead the British battlecruisers commanded by Vice-Admiral Beatty on to the guns of Scheer's battleships before Jellicoe could come to Beatty's aid.

Jellicoe set his own trap. Unknown to Scheer, his 24 Dreadnought battleships were steaming south from Scapa Flow on an interception course while Beatty's squadron of nine

Right: The man who could have lost the war in an afternoon – Admiral Sir John Jellicoe, commander of the British Grand Fleet. His indecision at Jutland aroused great controversy, but his prime aim was to preserve the Grand Fleet intact. His relations with his great rival Beatty were somewhat less than cordial.

Below: The battlecruiser *Queen Mary* (right) blows up at about 4.26pm. She had been hit several times and a cordite fire exploded her forward magazine. There were only 20 survivors of a crew of 58 officers and 1,228 men. Ahead of *Queen Mary* the battlecruiser *Tiger* is straddled by German shells. An observer in *Tiger* said of the end of *Queen Mary*: 'The whole ship seemed to collapse inwards. . . the roofs of the turrets [solid sheets of armour weighing 70 tons] were blown 100 feet high, then everything was smoke'.

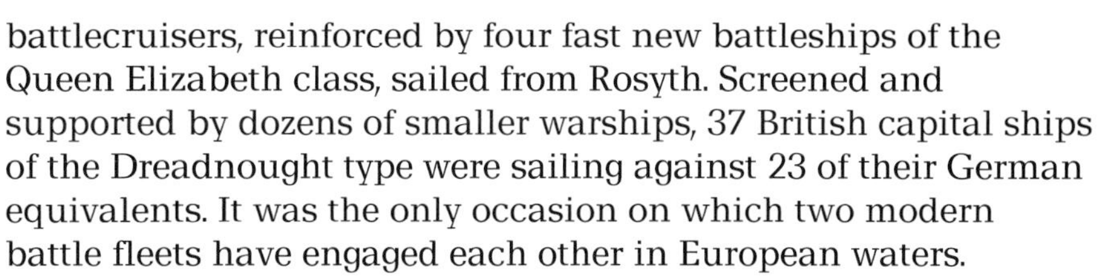

battlecruisers, reinforced by four fast new battleships of the Queen Elizabeth class, sailed from Rosyth. Screened and supported by dozens of smaller warships, 37 British capital ships of the Dreadnought type were sailing against 23 of their German equivalents. It was the only occasion on which two modern battle fleets have engaged each other in European waters.

In the first clash between the battlecruisers, which began at 3.48pm on 31 May, at a range of 18,000 yards, Beatty lost *Indefatigable* and *Queen Mary*. At 5.26pm he turned back towards Jellicoe in an attempt to lure Scheer on to the guns of the Grand Fleet. Scheer swiftly executed a 'battle turnaway', in the process of which another British battlecruiser, *Invincible*, was sunk. In rapidly fading light the two fleets blundered into each other again at 7.15pm. Once again threatened with destruction, Scheer withdrew to the west under the cover of a massed torpedo attack by his destroyers which forced Jellicoe to turn away to the east.

When daylight came Jellicoe found himself steaming across an empty sea. The British had lost three battlecruisers, three armoured cruisers and eight destroyers; the Germans lost one old battleship, one battlecruiser, four light cruisers and three destroyers. The Germans could claim a tactical success but the strategic advantage still lay with the Royal Navy as the Grand Fleet remained in being.

Admiral Franz von Hipper, commander of the German battlecruiser squadron at Jutland. The encounter demonstrated that the German ships were more battleworthy than their British counterparts, with heavier armour where it counted most and superior gunnery and fire control. At Jutland the Grand Fleet's largest losses in men and material were caused by inferior magazine protection.

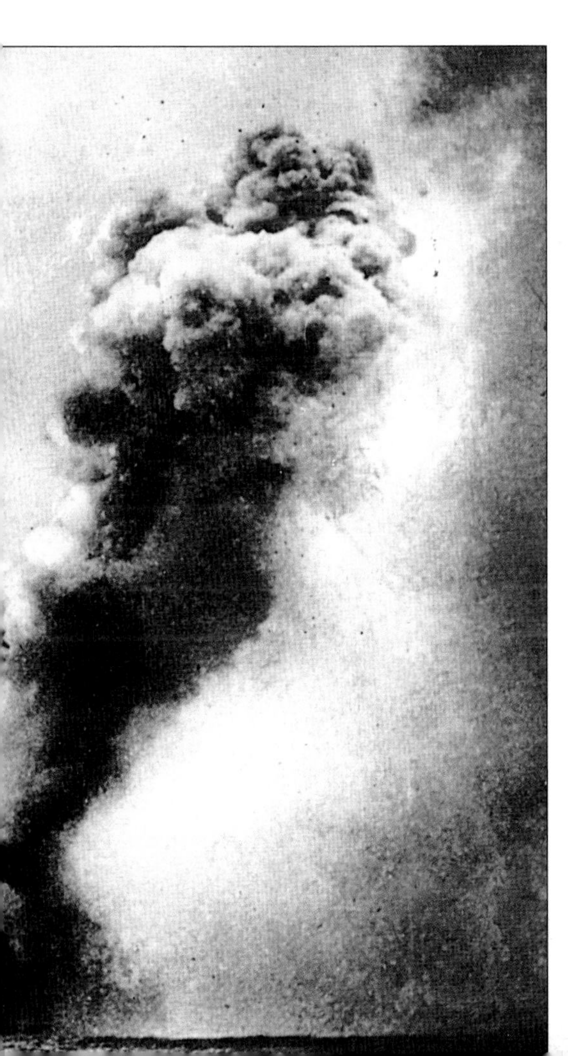

THE BATTLE OF THE ATLANTIC

BY 1914 GERMANY had a submarine fleet of about 70 U-boats. German admirals, and their British counterparts, initially saw the submarine as an auxiliary to their main fleets, acting as scouts and harrying battleships. Little attention was given to the submarine's potential against Britain's merchant shipping lifeline.

At the beginning of 1915 the German navy stepped up its U-boat operations after the declaration of a blockade on the British Isles. Surface hunters forced U-boat commanders to make periscope rather than surface attacks, a tactic which made it hard to identify neutral vessels. On 7 May a U-boat sank the British liner *Lusitania*, among whose 1,200 passengers were 124 Americans. Fear of drawing the United States into the war prompted the Germans to bring a halt to 'unrestricted' submarine warfare in September 1915.

Below: A German U-boat at sea. Submarines posed a powerful new threat, but they were defeated by a combination of the convoy system and new technology. By 1918 the Allied Submarine Detection Committe had invented a new submarine-tracking sonar device named after it – ASDIC. Of the 372 U-boats deployed during the war the Germans lost 192.

Deadlock on the Western Front led to renewed demands for the reinstatement of unrestricted submarine warfare. On 31 January 1917 the Germans announced that all shipping, including neutral vessels, would be sunk on sight in the war zone of the eastern Atlantic, the measure which brought the Americans into the war. This did not unduly trouble the German high command, which had calculated that Britain would be starved into submission in five months, before US intervention could be effective.

The U-boats nearly succeeded. In April 1917, the month the United States entered the war, they sank over a million tons of shipping. The answer, forced on an unwilling Admiralty by the British Prime Minister, Lloyd George, was the convoy system. In the vastness of the Atlantic, 100 ships sailing in convoy, were as difficult for a U-boat to locate as a ship sailing alone and unprotected. Losses to the U-boats fell dramatically while those inflicted on the submarines by new minefields and packs of hunter vessels rose steadily. By 1918 the average life expectancy of a U-boat based on the Flanders coast was only six voyages.

Above: Victim of the U-boats. The solution to the U-boat crisis was the convoy system. An experimental convoy was run from Gibraltar on 10 May 1917, and by November the system had become fully operational, forcing U-boats to make underwater attacks. Convoy escorts were able to locate U-boats with the assistance of increasingly reliable hydrophones and attack them with depth charges. Mines were also improved and claimed many U-boats.

Left: Funeral service for victims of the sinking of the *Lusitania* by a U-boat in May 1915. The Germans claimed that the liner was carrying large amounts of war material in her cargo. There is convincing evidence that on her last voyage the *Lusitania's* hold contained millions of rounds of ammunition and a quantity of explosive.

KITCHENER'S NEW ARMIES

BEFORE 1914 Britain had not possessed a mass army of the continental type. But Kitchener, the Secretary of State for War, had the insight to grasp at the outset that the war would last for several years. Victory over Germany would require the raising of a 'million army'.

Kitchener launched a personal appeal to British manhood. Everywhere his stern face stared out from posters, declaring *'Your Country Needs You'.* The response was overwhelming. In the next twelve months, 2.3 million men joined what became known as 'The New Army'. Thereafter, with the flow of volunteers drying up, conscription was introduced for men between 18 and 45.

Below: Joining up in London's Trafalgar Square. Many who flocked to join the colours were under age. One volunteer recalled: 'The sergeant asked me my age and when told replied, "Clear off, son, come back tomorrow and we'll see if you're 19, eh?" So I turned up the next day and gave my age as 19'. Men not in uniform were often taunted and presented with white feathers as a mark of cowardice.

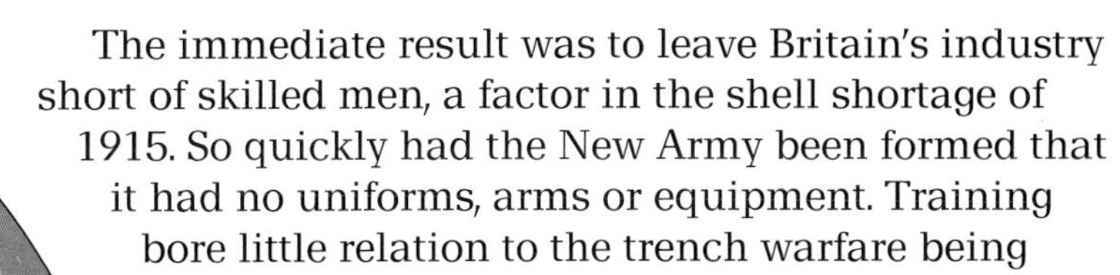

The immediate result was to leave Britain's industry short of skilled men, a factor in the shell shortage of 1915. So quickly had the New Army been formed that it had no uniforms, arms or equipment. Training bore little relation to the trench warfare being waged in France. The men of the New Armies got their first experience of the real thing in 1915, and were committed to action at the Battle of Loos in September of that year.

The new Army's inexperience had a baleful effect on British planning for the offensives of 1916. The New Army provided 97 of the 143 battalions which went over the top on 1 July 1916, the first day of the Battle of the Somme. Their commanders had no faith in their abilities. When the attack went in, no more was expected of them than a uniform parade-ground advance in successive waves across 'no man's land'.

Lord Kitchener (1850-1916), Secretary for War, 1914-16. Kitchener enjoyed wide-ranging powers, being both a minister and effectively Army chief until the curtailment of his powers after the Gallipoli fiasco in December 1915 when General Robertson was appointed Chief of the Imperial General Staff. Kitchener drowned on 5 June 1916 when the cruiser on which he was travelling to Russia struck a mine off the Orkneys.

Below: Doing their bit. Pupils at Eton drilling in 1915. Their time in the trenches would come.

VERDUN – THE CHARNEL HOUSE

IN THE winter of 1915 the attention of the German Chief of Staff, von Falkenhayn, turned to the French fortress system at Verdun, which had been virtually stripped of its guns and permanent garrisons. By forcing the French high command to defend this historic bastion to the last man, he hoped to *'bleed France white'* with guns rather than men.

On 21 February 1916 the Germans opened their assault with a bombardment of unparalleled ferocity. Four days later, as General Henri Pétain, arrived to command French forces in the sector, with orders to contest every shell-churned inch of ground, the virtually undefended Fort Douaumont fell to a patrol of Brandenburgers.

During the next three months no fewer than 78 French divisions went into the mincing machine at Verdun, fed down the only road not closed by German artillery, the 'Sacred Way', along which 6,000 trucks passed every day. The French stabilized their defences and the Germans began to substitute men for munitions. Now they were being bled white. By the end of April their losses were exceeding those of the French. The German effort was halted at the end of June, when the British bombardment began on the Somme and the Russians attacked on the Eastern Front. In the autumn, when the fighting at Verdun seemed to be over, General Robert Nivelle, who had replaced the promoted Pétain in April, launched a series of lightning counter-strokes which regained all the lost ground with very few casualties. Small consolation,perhaps, for the 500,000 the French had sustained in the defence of Verdun.

General Erich von Falkenhayn, Chief of German Staff, September 1914-August 1916, the architect of the strategy of attrition against the French at Verdun. His failure resulted in his replacement by Hindenburg, after which Falkenhayn commanded forces in Romania in 1916 and then in the Caucasus and Palestine.

Left: A French infantryman falls at Verdun. A French sergeant who fought in the battle described the agonizing effort needed to go over the top: 'What a hideous thing; to say to oneself, at this moment I am myself; my blood circulates and pulses in my arteries; I have my eyes, all my skin is intact, I do not bleed! . . . Oh, to be able to sleep thinking that it is finished, that I shall live, that I shall not be killed!'

Below: German prisoners taken at Verdun. Overall German casualties during the battle were 440,000. For French and Germans alike, Verdun 'meant hell. No fields. No woods. Just a lunar landscape. Roads cratered. Trenches staved in, filled up, remade, redug, filled in again. The snow has melted; the shellholes are full of water. The wounded drown in them. A man can no longer drag himself out of the mud'.

SACRIFICE ON THE SOMME

IN DECEMBER 1915 the British and French began to lay plans for a big joint offensive on the Somme, where their lines met. For most of the war this had been a quiet sector where battalions had, on occasion, drilled undisturbed on open fields in full view of the enemy.

After the exhausting struggle at Verdun, the burden of the fighting in this sector was to be shouldered by the British Third and Fourth Armies. Their extensive preparations were noted by the Germans, who strengthened their front-line defences to meet the attack announced by a massive bombardment which began on 24 June 1916.

The British high command confidently expected that the bombardment, which expended over 1.5 million shells – many of which were duds – would break up the German barbed wire, bludgeon their batteries into silence and entomb the defenders in their dug-outs. They were wrong on all counts. At 7.30am on the broiling hot morning of 1 July the bombardment moved on to the German second line. The German machine gunners emerged from their dug-outs, shaken but unscathed, to pour a withering fire into the 13 British divisions advancing at a walking pace across 'no man's land'.

Below: Irish troops rest in a communications trench on the first day on the Somme. Irish formations were heavily involved that day, and four Irishmen won the Victoria Cross, three of them posthumously. The Ulster Divison captured a long section of the German front line at Thiepval and fought its way through to the German second line before being driven back.

Right: Men of the Tyneside Irish Brigade going over the top near La Boisselle on 1 July. Advancing over open ground, the Brigade's 3,000 men were cut to shreds by machine-gun fire. Sergeant J. Galloway remembered: 'I could see, away to my left and right, long lines of men. Then I heard the patter-patter of machine-guns in the distance. By the time I'd gone another ten yards there seemed to be only a few men left around me; by the time I had gone 20 yards, I seemed to be on my own. Then I was hit myself'.

By nightfall the British had lost 60,000 men, 19,000 of them dead. The offensive ground on, making only minor gains. On 15 September British tanks were used to pierce the German line south of Bapaume, but there was no breakthrough, only autumn rain and seas of mud. The Battle of the Somme ended on 18 November, by which time the British had suffered some 420,000 casualties and the Germans a similar number. All idealism about the conduct of the war died on the Somme.

Above: British and German wounded on their way to a dressing station during the fighting near Montauban on 19 July.

THE HOME FRONT

IN 1914 there was a widespread feeling that, in spite of the war, it would be 'Business as Usual' back in Britain. In the next four years, however, the demands of war brought important social changes.

The massive exodus of men from the factories and mines to join Kitchener's New Army left Britain's industry short of skilled labour. In the factories their places were, in large part, filled by women, an important step on the road to female emancipation. During the war women moved into many areas of traditional male employment. A soldier returning to 'Blighty' on leave would be struck by women working on the railways as porters and guards and on the trams as conductors. Members of the Women's Land Army helped to boost agricultural output.

There were problems, however. In spite of government pledges, women war workers earned less than men. Trade unionists claimed that the employment of so many women in industry – in some munitions plants they outnumbered the male workforce by three to one – would lower mens' wages.

Below: A woman at work in an engineering factory. The war was a total conflict in that it forced the combatant nations to transform their societies, economies and even their political structures. It demanded the total mobilization of the state's resources on an unprecedented scale, which led to increased intervention in all aspects of its citizens' lives. This ranged from relatively minor matters, like the introduction of licensing laws and summer time in Britain – as ways on increasing agricultural and industrial output – to the direction of labour under the provisions of the Defence of the Realm Act.

During the war the price of staple foods climbed steeply. In 1914-15 the price of meat rose by 40 per cent and that of sugar by nearly 70 per cent, prompting accusations that 'profiteers' were exploiting the situation to make fortunes. Later the U-boat campaign threatened Britain's Atlantic supply lines, but the rationing of sugar, meat and butter was not introduced until February 1918. In 1915 the government acted more swiftly to introduce licensing laws, to restrict the hours when public houses could open, after it was claimed that well-paid munitions workers were drinking away their afternoons.

Below: The ration cards issued to King George V and Queen Mary. The King also attempted to set a good example to his subjects by giving up drink for the duration of the war and turning the royal estates over to crop production.

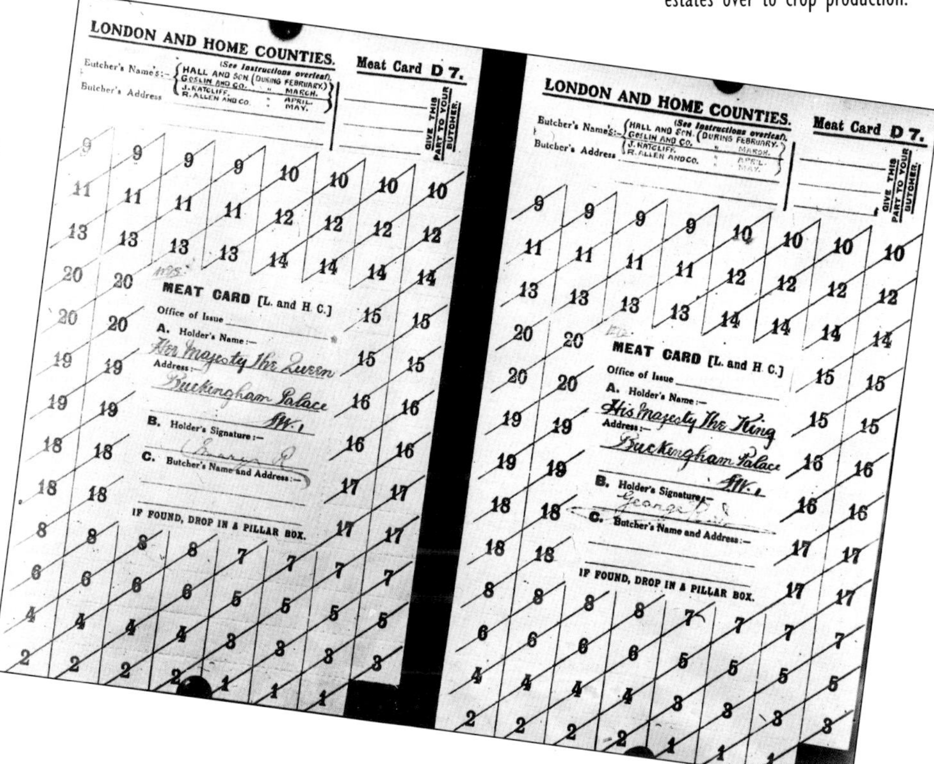
LONDON AND HOME COUNTIES. Meat Card D 7.

Butcher's Name's:— (See instructions overleaf.) HALL AND SON (DURING FEBRUARY) GOSLIN AND CO. " MARCH. J. KATCLIFF. " APRIL. R. ALLEN AND CO. " MAY.

Butcher's Address

GIVE THIS PART TO YOUR BUTCHER.

MEAT CARD [L. and H. C.]

Office of Issue

A. Holder's Name:— Her Majesty the Queen

Address:— Buckingham Palace S.W.

B. Holder's Signature:—

C. Butcher's Name and Address:—

IF FOUND, DROP IN A PILLAR BOX.

LONDON AND HOME COUNTIES. Meat Card D 7.

Butcher's Name's:— (See instructions overleaf.) HALL AND SON (DURING FEBRUARY) GOSLIN AND CO. " MARCH. J. KATCLIFF. " APRIL. R. ALLEN AND CO. " MAY.

Butcher's Address

GIVE THIS PART TO YOUR BUTCHER.

MEAT CARD [L. and H. C.]

Office of Issue

A. Holder's Name:— His Majesty the King

Address:— Buckingham Palace S.W.

B. Holder's Signature:— George

C. Butcher's Name and Address:—

IF FOUND, DROP IN A PILLAR BOX.

Below: Members of the Women's Land Army photographed in March 1918.

THE WAR IN THE AIR

THE SIMPLE statement, on the outbreak of war, that *'The squadrons flew to France'*, marked the end of secure British isolation from Continental Europe and foreshadowed a new form of warfare.

Sixty-three fragile but inherently stable aircraft of the Royal Flying Corps (RFC) accompanied the British Expeditionary Force. Their role, that of reconnaissance, was to remain the principal operational activity of the combatant air forces throughout the war. Air fighting began when bolder souls went aloft armed with carbines, darts and even bricks, to ensure that their duties were uninterrupted.

In February 1915 two Frenchmen, Roland Garros and Raymond Saulnier, experimented with a forward-firing machine gun, fixing steel plates to the propeller of their aircraft to deflect the small percentage of bullets they calculated would hit it. In April, Garros came down behind German lines and his captured aircraft enabled the Dutch-born aero-engineer Anthony Fokker to produce a mechanical interrupter gear, which allowed the gun to fire only when no propeller blade was in the way. It was fitted to the Eindecker monoplane, which thus became the first true fighter aircraft.

Right: RFC aircrew report after a mission over enemy lines. The spotting of targets from the air, and the ranging of artillery on them with the aid of airborne wireless sets, was the primary preoccupation of the Allied and German air services as long as artillery support was deemed essential in any attempt to achieve a breakthrough. The prevailing westerly winds placed the RFC at a permanent tactical disadvantage, taking a heavy toll of battle-damaged or malfunctioning aircraft struggling back to Allied lines.

Below: A British reconnaissance aircraft touches down at sunset.

Above: Aerial photography made rapid strides. By March 1915 the RFC had assembled a complete photographic picture of the German trench system opposite British First Army at Neuve Chapelle to a depth of 1,500 yards. Details of the German defences were traced on a map, 1,500 copies of which were issued to each corps taking part in the attack on 10 March.

ZEPPELIN

IN THE World Crisis, Winston Churchill wrote that from the beginning of the war there was a widespread fear that *'at any moment half a dozen Zeppelins might arrive to bomb London, or what was more serious, Chatham, Woolwich or Portsmouth'.*

In 1914 the German armed forces had 30 rigid airships, all of them of the Zeppelin type named after their designer Count Ferdinand von Zeppelin. Although their most effective role throughout the war was that of maritime reconnaissance, it was not long before the Zeppelins were employed on bombing operations, first on the Western Front and then against the British Isles.

The first effective Zeppelin raid on London was launched by the German Navy's Airship Division on 8 September 1915, when L13 penetrated London's primitive air defences to drop its bombs in a line running from Euston to Liverpool Street, killing 26 people. Following this, and later Zeppelin raids on London, much damage to property was done in anti-German riots. By the end of the war, 51 bombing raids by airships had been made against England, killing 557 people.

In spite of their size – the 'super-Zeppelins' introduced in 1916 were 650ft long – the airships proved fragile instruments of war, difficult to navigate with any accuracy, and vulnerable both to the elements and to fighters armed with incendiary bullets. By the end of the war over 60 of the German armed forces' 88 Zeppelins had been lost, 34 to accidents caused by bad weather and the rest to Allied aircraft and ground fire. Nevertheless, they exerted a powerful psychological effect and diverted significant resources to the air defence of Britain which would otherwise have been employed in France.

Above: Sentries guard the wreckage of Zeppelin L31, shot down over Potter's Bar on 1 October 1916 by a British BE2c piloted by Second Lieutenant Wulstan Tempest, who saw the airship's hull 'go red inside like an enormous Chinese lantern'.

Left: LZ95, a German Army Zeppelin used on the Western Front, where she was written off in 1916 after being hit by French shell fire and crashing near Namur. Note the forward gun turret on the upper hull, where the silhouetted figures indicate the huge size of the Zeppelin.

Right: Anti-German riots in London's East End after Zeppelin raids in the autumn of 1915.

THE FIGHTER ACES

IN THE hands of pilots like Max Immelmann and Oswald Boelcke, the Eindeckers took a heavy toll of relatively defenceless Allied aircraft. Boelcke, who claimed 40 victories, codified the basic techniques of air combat in a pithy set of rules for pilots, the 'Dicta Boelcke', which were still being issued, in booklet form, to Luftwaffe pilots in World War II.

Boelcke also drew on his experience in the fierce aerial fighting over Verdun in February-June 1916 to form specialized fighting squadrons, the Jagdstaffeln (hunting flights), known as Jastas. An early recruit to Jasta 2, commanded by Boelcke, was Freiherr Manfred von Richthofen, the top-scoring ace of the war with 80 victories.

With the arrival of new aircraft types, the Allies began to produce their own fighter aces, among them the frail-looking French Capitaine Georges Guynemer of Escadrille N3 and the RFC's youthful Captain Albert Ball, who flew with 11 Squadron. Like many aces they adopted 'lone wolf' tactics, undeterred by the frequently heavy odds against them. However, by 1917 air fighting had overwhelmingly become a matter of teamwork based on formation flying.

Above: Oswald Boelcke, the father of fighter pilot tactics. He claimed 40 victories before being shot down and killed on 25 October 1916 while leading Jasta 2, which subsequently became known as 'Jasta Boelcke'. Boelcke's contemporary fame was overshadowed by that of his friend Max Immelmann, the 'Eagle of Lille', who shot down 17 Allied aircraft in his Eindecker before meeting his end on 15 June 1916.

Left: The French ace Georges Guynemer, earthbound and surrounded by an infantry escort at a flag dedication ceremony. By 1917 the frail Guynemer was France's leading ace, flying Spad S VIIs with the elite Cigognes (storks) Group. He scored his 54th and final official victory on 6 September 1917; five days later he failed to return from a mission, possibly having been hit by ground fire. His Spad crashed during a barrage and both aircraft and national hero were obliterated by the shelling.

Left: The fabled 'Red Baron', Rittmeister Manfred Freiherr von Richthofen. He shot down more aircraft than any other pilot of World War I – 80 in all – and was a supreme professional in a new and deadly profession. He gained his nickname from the red-painted Fokker DrI triplane which he often flew and in which he was killed on 21 April 1918, shot down by a Sopwith Camel piloted by Flight Commander A.R. Brown of 209 Squadron, RFC.

Below: The Albatros biplanes of Jasta 11, von Richthofen's 'Flying Circus', which boasted some of the finest fighter pilots of the war. By the spring of 1917 the Albatros D III was being flown by all of Germany's front-line fighter units and was inflicting heavy casualties on the RFC. It was not until the autumn of 1917 that its performance was overhauled by new Allied fighters like the Sopwith Camel and the French Spad VII.

THE EASTERN FRONT

IN MARCH 1915 the Russians resumed the offensive in Galicia and took the great fortress of Przemysl. Their success forced the German Chief of Staff, Falkenhayn, to turn his attention to the Eastern Front. If he could decisively defeat the Russians, he could then bring superior forces to bear on the Allies in the West.

In May the Germans and Austrians attacked on a 28-mile front at Gorlice, driving the Russians out of most of Poland and taking nearly a million prisoners. The Russians held on, retreating 300 miles before halting the Germans on a new defensive line. The Tsar dismissed the Grand Duke Nicholas as Commander-in-Chief and took command himself.

In June 1916 the Russians were ready to attack again. Their drive on Warsaw came to grief, but south of the Pripet marshes General Alexei Brusilov unleashed a surprise offensive along a 300-mile front against the Austrian Fourth and Seventh Armies. Dispensing with a concentration of troops and a preliminary bombardment, he simply attacked wherever he could. In two weeks he took 200,000 prisoners.

Above: Tsar Nicholas II inspects a Cossack guard of honour. In 1915 the Germans put out feelers to the Tsar, suggesting a peace settlement on the basis of the status quo. Nicholas II, fearful that his authority might be undermined by anything less than total victory, remained loyal to his French allies. Russia remained trapped by the war, unable to win it and unable to escape from it.

Right: Russian infantry rest in a captured German trench. The Russian victories of the summer of 1916 were born of necessity. Lacking sufficient ammunition, Brusilov had relied on suprise, little or no preliminary bombardment and a series of separate attacks on a wide front to confuse the enemy as to his intentions. But he did not have the reserves to exploit the breakthrough.

Left: German troops march through a Russian town. In 1915, just as in 1914, the Germans achieved a series of spectacular victories on the Eastern Front, bundling the Russians out of Poland and taking 750,000 prisoners in the process. However, as General Brusilov demonstrated in the summer of 1916, the Russian Army remained a threat.

By the end of the summer, German reinforcements diverted from the attack on Verdun, and Russian shortage of ammunition and reserves, had shut down Brusilov's offensive. It had effectively undermined Austria as a military power but had also cost Russia nearly a million casualties, losses which accelerated the collapse which was to lead to the Russian Revolution.

THE ITALIAN FRONT

ITALY DECLARED war on Austria-Hungary on 23 May 1915. The main area of fighting was in the sector of the Isonzo River, west of Trieste, where strong Austrian forces were deployed in excellent mountain defences. The Italians battered away at them in a long series of offensives collectively known as the Battles of the Isonzo, but it was not until the eleventh offensive in August-September 1917, that they broke through the Austrian line.

German aid arrived in the form of Fourteenth Austrian Army, comprising mainly German troops, whose infiltration tactics secured victory in the twelfth Battle of the Isonzo, also known as Caporetto, in October-November 1917. By 12 November the Italians had been driven back to the River Piave, where the Austro-German advance was halted by a shortage of supplies and the arrival of 11 British and French divisions under the able General Plumer. Nevertheless, Italian losses were some 400,000 men, 350,000 taken prisoner.

Below: Italian gunners provide their Austrian opponents with a deadly form of Easter egg. By mid-September 1916, Italian artillery were pounding away in the seventh Battle of the Isonzo, which lasted well into November.

German troops in Italy were transferred to the Western Front for Ludendorff's last throw in 1918, leaving the Austrians to punch themselves out in a renewed offensive launched in June. The Austrian-Hungarian empire was tottering into oblivion, and its high command desperately seeking an armistice in Italy, when at the beginning of November it suffered its final military defeat at Vittorio Veneto.

Below: Austrian troops in action on the Isonzo front. At the Battle of Caporetto, Austro-German forces used new infiltration tactics which drove the Italians back to the Piave. A young German officer who distinguished himself during the battle, winning a Pour le Mérite, was a certain Erwin Rommel.

Below: German machine-gunners in Italy, 1917. The German helmet, the Stalhelm, was first issued to troops at Verdun in January 1916, but another year passed before it became standard issue. It weighed about two and a half pounds. The French helmet was introduced in 1915 and the British in February 1916.

THE NIVELLE OFFENSIVE

AFTER HIS success at Verdun, General Nivelle succeeded Joffre as the French C-in-C, promising to end the war with one swift blow of *'violence, brutality and rapidity'*. He found an eager ally in the British Prime Minister David Lloyd George, who enlisted Nivelle in his own private war with the British C-in-C, Sir Douglas Haig.

The Allied plans for a joint offensive in the spring of 1917, with the British high command reluctantly placing itself under French orders, was dislocated by the German withdrawal to the heavily fortified Hindenburg Line, which began on 16 March. Brimming with self-confidence which bordered on the pathological, Nivelle ignored the changed circumstances. His strategy remained unmodified when the offensive began on 16 April on a 40-mile front east of Soissons.

Before the battle began, Nivelle had predicted 10,000 casualties as the price of victory. In the first four days the French Fifth and Sixth Armies suffered 120,000 casualties. Nivelle's attempts to persist with his broken-backed offensive shattered the spirit of the French Army – already weakened by the sacrifices made at Verdun – and led to a widespread mutiny. Within a month, 54 divisions, half the French Army, could no longer be counted upon by its high command.

Right: The man who talked too much. General Robert Nivelle, still jaunty on a visit to New York in 1920. He made no attempt to preserve the secrecy of his offensive, and the Germans, armed with a captured set of French plans, prepared their defence in depth.

Right: French troops go over the top. In the opening phase of the Nivelle offensive they displayed great dash and courage in appalling weather conditions. But once again the German machine-guns had survived the opening bombardment to mow down whole waves of French infantry. The French gained four miles at the point of greatest effort, but no one believed that this was the decisive victory promised by the loquacious Nivelle.

Left: French prisoners of war after the Nivelle offensive. The effort they had made was about to prove too much.

MUTINY

IN THE spring of 1917, after the failure of Nivelle's futile offensive in Champagne, the French Army was rapidly reaching the end of its tether. For many units, leave had all but ceased and desertions had more than doubled. Pétain wrote gloomily, *'Hopelessness and pessimism spread . . . swamping as it did the mood of artificial enthusiasm whipped up from above . . .'*

In May 1917 isolated acts of protest and indiscipline flared into open mutiny. By the end of the month it was estimated that only two of the 12 divisions in Champagne

Below: At the end of his tether – a hero of Verdun. The ten-month battle took a terrible psychological toll. A young French officer killed at Verdun had written in his diary: 'They will not be able to make us do it again another day'.

could be relied upon – and none of those between Paris and Soissons. Astonishingly, the Germans remained unaware of the crisis gripping the French Army. The task of restoring order was given to Pétain, who employed a mixture of brute force and concessions. He restricted the death penalty to the worst offenders, of whom 55 faced the firing squad, although many more were summarily executed. He also formed disciplinary companies for those found guilty of mutiny, assigning them the most hazardous of duties.

Pétain also improved communications between headquarters and the men at the front, as well as increasing pay and enhancing conditions for his troops. Above all, Pétain put into practice his theory of wearing down the enemy with limited, inexpensive attacks. This package of measures hauled the Army back from the brink of disintegration and prepared it for the German offensives in 1918.

Below: French infantry – the legendary poilus – examine their mail. The improvement of conditions at the front played an important part in rallying the French Army. On 2 June all troops were guaranteed seven days leave every four months, later extended to ten days. Food was improved as were the facilities in rest areas. On 3 August an order was placed for the immediate delivery of half a million beds to the rest areas.

Below: French infantry in action in June 1917 at a time when few of them could be relied on to obey orders. By the end of May over 55 separate mutinies had swept through the French Army. The men who had not left their posts held the line but refused to attack. To cover their ally, the British were forced to continue their offensive at Arras, originally launched on 9 April as a diversionary measure in support of Nivelle's attack. The British 'diversion' eventually cost them 158,000 casualties.

THE GERMAN HOME FRONT

THE DEMANDS of war – its greed for guns and shells – created an industrial revolution. New industries sprang up to feed the war machine, and with them new systems of working and new social problems: food shortages and rocketing prices, resentment at 'profiteers' and the maintenance of the wives and families of men serving in the armed forces.

Germans blamed the food shortages they endured throughout the war on the distant naval blockade maintained by the British. Unlike Britain, however, Germany had imported little or no food before the war. The main problem was caused by the departure of millions of men from the land into the army. In 1916 there was a bad harvest followed by a bitter winter, the so-called 'turnip winter', in which root crops became the staple diet.

The food shortage concerned Hindenburg and Ludendorff, who by 1916 were the most powerful figures in Germany. Ludendorff presided over the establishment of a new body, the Kriegsamt, which organized the civilian manpower of Germany for war. In theory it could conscript all male labour between 18 and 60. In practice it bribed workers with higher wages.

But the food shortages haunted Germany to the end of the war. In October 1918 a member of the German government wrote: '*We have no meat, potatoes cannot be delivered because we are short of 4,000 trucks a day. Fat is unobtainable. The shortage is so great that it is a mystery to me what the people of Berlin live on. The workers say, "Better a horrible end than an endless horror"*'.

Below: Distributing bread in Vienna.

Left: In 1915, when hopes of decisive victory still ran high, crowds of civilians throng the Savings Bank of Charlottenburg as they subscribe to a War Loans drive. Each subscriber could hammer a nail into a huge wooden statue of Hindenburg. Significantly, none of the combatant nations attempted to pay for the war by raising taxes. Germany even reduced taxes to lighten the hardships of war. It was assumed that, in the final count, the defeated enemy would pay.

Below: Women and hungry-looking children join a ration queue in 1916.

THE YANKS ARE COMING!

WHEN Woodrow Wilson narrowly won a second term as US President in November 1916, the slogan of his Party, the Democrats, had been *'He kept us out of the war'*. However, American isolation was not to last much longer.

Unrestricted German submarine warfare drew the United States into the war. On 31 January 1917 Germany announced that all shipping, including that of neutrals, would be sunk on sight by U-boats in the Atlantic war zone. On 2 February Wilson broke off relations with Germany. The U-boats immediately began sinking US ships. Shortly afterwards, American newspapers revealed a German scheme, outlined in the 'Zimmerman telegram', to help the Mexicans recover New Mexico from the United States. Reluctantly, Woodrow Wilson declared war on Germany on 6 April 1917.

Below: General Pershing and George V inspect American troops. As the US military attaché to Tokyo, 'Black Jack' Pershing had observed the Russo-Japanese War of 1905-6. In 1916 he had commanded a force of 10,000 men sent into Mexico during the Mexican Revolution in pursuit of Pancho Villa. Pursuing the Kaiser as commander of the American Expeditionary Force was a more taxing undertaking.

Right: American troops receive a friendly welcome in London in August 1917. It would be many months before they went into action in France. At this stage in the war, American money loans were more useful than men. But the United States' entry into the conflict provided the Allies with a huge boost to morale and the hope of victory in 1918.

America's entry into the war brought almost unbounded manpower and material resources to the Allies, but it would take time for them to be mobilised. In France the American build-up was painfully slow. By 1 May 1918 there were scarcely eight US divisions in France, the bulk of them unprepared for action. Their commander, General John Joseph Pershing, wanted to form them into a separate Army Group and was reluctant to see his small force dissipated by detachments to help the British and French forces staggering under the impact of the Ludendorff offensive launched in the previous March.

Below: Baptism of fire: A confident column of American troops marches past battle-weary British infantry on 19 May 1918, ten days before US formations got their first taste of combat on the Western Front.

THE SIDE SHOWS

THE FIRST World War was a global conflict. The Central Powers, represented by Germany, Austria-Hungary, Turkey and Bulgaria, were eventually opposed by no fewer than 22 Allied countries, including Japan, Portugal and the United States.

The war spilled far beyond the Eastern and Western Fronts in Europe. Even within Europe there was the war between Austria-Hungary and Italy after the latter joined the Allies in May 1915. In October 1915, in an attempt to help the Serbs, an Anglo-French force landed at Salonika to open a separate Balkan front against Bulgaria. By 1917, nearly 600,000 Allied troops were tied down in this dead-end theatre, which the Germans sardonically dubbed the 'greatest Allied internment camp of the war'.

The Allied war against Turkey embraced the Dardanelles campaign of 1915, the Russian campaign in the Caucasus and the British campaigns in Egypt, Palestine and Mesopotamia. Campaigns were also waged in the German colonies of the Cameroons, Togoland and German South West and East Africa. In the latter, the brilliant German General von Lettow-Vorbeck, commanding only 4,000 men, tied down a British force of 140,000 in a four-year guerrilla war. A succession of frustrated British generals failed to get the better of Lettow-Vorbeck, who surrendered 12 days after the Armistice in November 1918.

Right: General von Lettow-Vorbeck (centre right), the German commander in East Africa, relaxes over a bottle or two of Bols. A commander of the highest calibre, Lettow-Vorbeck ran rings round his numerically superior enemy in a campaign in which the tropical, disease-ridden climate claimed the greater part of casualties on both sides.

Below: A battalion of Nigerian troops entrain at Lagos on 6 August 1914. They played a part in achieving a swift victory over German forces in the Togoland and the Cameroons.

Below: Serbian infantry outside Belgrade. The Serbian incursion into Austro-Hungarian territory ended in the autumn of 1915. In October, Bulgaria attacked Serbia. Under the combined weight of Austro-German and Bulgarian offensives, Serbia collapsed and her army took refuge first in Albania, then in Corfu. The Bulgarians went on to defeat the Anglo-French force in Macedonia and bottle it up in Salonika, where it was subsequently reinforced by the Serbian divisions from Corfu, the Russians and the Italians.

ENTER THE TANK

Below: Not the perfect weapon of war. A British tank abandoned during the Arras offensive in the spring of 1917. Only 60 tanks were available for the battle, and ground conditions prevented many of them from seeing action. To the end of the war the tank laboured under severe technical limitations. It was prone to mechanical failure, vulnerable to artillery fire and too slow to exploit a breakthrough. The Germans thoroughly distrusted tanks and made no significant attempt to use them until 24 April 1918, when they employed 13 at Villers Brettoneux. This action also saw the first tank-versus-tank encounter, when three British Mk IVs engaged three German A7Vs.

IN OCTOBER 1914 the official British war correspondent Colonel Ernest Swinton approached General Headquarters (GHQ) with a proposal to use the pre-war Holt agricultural steam tractor as a means of overcoming barbed wire and broken ground.

GHQ was not interested but Swinton's scheme eventually found a backer in Winston Churchill, First Lord of the Admiralty. In the autumn of 1914 armoured cars operated in northern France by the Royal Naval Air Service (RNAS) had enjoyed some success but had been hampered by trenches which the Germans had dug across the roads. The Admiralty's work on a solution to this problem coincided with Swinton's proposal and led to the establishment of an Admiralty Landships Committee in February 1915.

A series of trials led to a prototype armoured vehicle known as 'Big Willie' which was successfully tested at Hatfield Park at the beginning of 1916. Kitchener dismissed 'Big Willie' as a *'pretty mechanical toy'* but Haig was keen to use the machines – codenamed 'tanks' – in France as soon as possible. They were first employed in significant numbers on 15 September 1916, during the Battle of the Somme, but were thrown forward in uncoordinated fashion. It was not until November 1917 that the tanks were successfully employed *en masse* at Cambrai.

Left: Another casualty of the Battle of Arras. At Cambrai on 20 November 1917, the British used tanks en masse for the first time. After a lightning bombardment, 324 fighting tanks, using specially devised tactics, tore a six-mile gap in the Hindenburg Line. Once again, however, the breakthrough was not exploited and most of the ground gained was lost to a fierce German counterattack launched on 30 November.

Below: Mk V tanks and men of the Australian Fifth Division move up in the assault on the Hindenburg Line in 1918. The 'male' versions of the Mk V were armed with a short 6-pounder gun and a Hotchkiss machine-gun. Top speed was about 4.5mph.

THEY CALLED IT PASSCHENDAELE

ALSO KNOWN as the third Battle of Ypres, Passchendaele remains the symbol of the seemingly futile carnage of the Western Front and the obstinacy of the the British C-in-C, Sir Douglas Haig.

Learning nothing from the failure on the Somme in 1916, Haig now planned a purely British offensive in the Ypres salient, with the aim of driving to Ostend to capture the enemy's submarine bases and sever the Belgian railways on which German communications depended. Haig's intelligence staff voiced their misgivings about the waterlogged ground over which he was to fight, but on 25 July 1917 he informed the British War Cabinet that all was ready.

Below: A 9.2-in howitzer in action, November 1917. The Passchendaele offensive, officially known as the Third Battle of Ypres, took the form of eight separate attempts to extend the Ypres salient between 31 July and 19 November 1918. Siegrfried Sasson wrote of it:

'I died in hell –
(They called it Passchendaele);
my wound was slight
And I was hobbling back, and then a shell
Burst slick upon the duck-boards; so I fell
Into the bottomless mud, and lost the light'.

Below: Infantry pick their way through the sodden earth near Pilckem Ridge on 16 August. Driving rain and strong German counterattacks through oceans of mud brought the first phase of the British offensive to a grinding halt.

The Germans had ample warning of the offensive. By the time the attack went in on 31 July there were nearly two million combatants crammed into the Ypres salient. Haig's preliminary bombardment destroyed the area's fragile drainage system and his 13 infantry divisions advanced into a morass. The attack ground on until the beginning of November, with progress being measured in hundreds of yards, before it was halted only five miles from the original start line. Each mile had cost 50,000 casualties.

Below: Australian troops at Château Wood. In September and early October masterful use of British artillery in step-by-step blows, and the vigour of Australian and New Zealand infantry divisions, made significant gains. Then the rain intervened again in drenching torrents turning the battlefield to porridge and forcing the abandonment of the offensive.

THE MIDDLE EAST

GALLIPOLI WAS not the only disaster the British suffered in their war against Turkey. At the end of 1915 General Townshend's advance on Baghdad was fought to a halt by stubborn Turkish resistance, and his force of 10,000 British and Indian troops bottled up in Kut-al-Amara. In April 1916 he surrendered. Baghdad was not taken until March 1917.

Greater success was achieved in Palestine, where General Allenby replaced General Murray as commander of British forces in April 1917. Allenby's instructions were to *'take Jerusalem by Christmas'*. This he duly achieved, entering the Holy City on 9 December.

In September 1918, Allenby renewed the offensive against the Fourth, Seventh and Eighth Turkish Armies (each of which was no larger than a division) under the overall command of the German General Liman von Sanders. At Megiddo, Allenby employed a brilliant deception plan, overwhelming air power and a strong cavalry force to achieve a victory which was not only comprehensive but also a rare example of surprise and mobility in a war dominated by barbed wire and the machine gun. Damascus was occupied on 10 October, and Turkey capitulated three weeks later.

Left: Irregular warrior. Colonel T.E. Lawrence, who in 1917-18 operated with a small group of other British officers alongside the Arabs against the Turks. Lawrence organized raiding parties attacking the Hejaz railway which isolated the city of Medina and obliged the Turks to divert 25,000 troops. The Arab Revolt laid the ground for Allenby's offensive of September 1918. Lawrence and his Arab allies entered Damascus at the end of the month. A complex figure, prone to fantasy, Lawrence was nevertheless a discerning theorist of guerrilla warfare, describing his exploits in 'The Seven Pillars of Wisdom'.

Above: RFC aircraft on an airstrip in Palestine in December 1917. Air power played an important part in the climax to the campaign in the Middle East. Having gained air supremacy over the German squadrons in the theatre, the bombers of the Palestine Brigade struck at enemy communications and headquarters. The Brigade's fighter-bombers then bombed and strafed enemy columns. Turkish Seventh and Eighth Armies were caught in defiles blocked with smashed guns and vehicles and then systematically destroyed. The Turkish Fourth Army, unscathed but in open country east of the Jordan, also took heavy punishment from the Brigade's Bristol Fighters, DH9s and SE5As.

Right: General Allenby enters Jerusalem, December 1917.

THE COMMANDERS

THE WAR threw up a number of formidable military figures but none of them was a commander of the first rank. All of them, however, laboured under two signal disadvantages. The First Word War was the only war ever fought in which commanders lacked voice control over their armies. Communications broke down almost immediately the troops left the trenches. The trenches themselves provided almost insuperable obstacles, not least because the commanders were caught by a fatal hiatus in the mobile arm. Horsed cavalry was quickly revealed as obsolete, while the tank had not yet been developed into the weapon which proved so decisive in the Battle of France in 1940. For most of the war defence was mechanized; attack was not.

On the German side, the dominating figure was that of Ludendorff, the victor of Tannenberg in 1914. He proved less successful on the Western Front from 1917, although his spring offensive of 1918 came close to success. At a lower level the Central Powers fielded excellent fighting generals in von Mackensen, the conqueror of Rumania; Liman von Sanders, who masterminded the defence of the Gallipoli peninsula in 1915; and von Lettow-Vorbeck, whose skilful defence of German East Africa against overwhelming odds earned him the distinction of being accorded the 'honours of war' when he was forced to capitulate.

Germany's warlords, Hindenburg and Ludendorff, in suitably forbidding mood. From 1916 they were the two most powerful men in Germany, symbols of the abandonment of the direction of the war by the politicians who had started it. Hindenburg served as President of Germany from 1925 to 1934, appointing Adolf Hitler as Chancellor in January 1933. Hitler became President when Hindenburg died in August 1934. Ludendorff was involved in Hitler's abortive Munich putsch in 1923 but later fell out with the Nazi leader.

Left: Pétain (left) and Joffre. The latter blocked the issue of steel helmets to the French Army in 1914 because he believed that the war would not last long enough for mass production to begin. Joffre was dimissed in December 1916 and shuffled off into the obscurity of an advisory role to the General Staff. Pétain succeeded the disgraced Nivelle as commander of the French Army and in 1918 became a Marshal of France. Pétain's postwar political career reached an inglorious climax as leader of the Vichy government during the German occupation in World War II.

For the French, Joffre's massive imperturbability, rather than any great insight as a commander, saw France through the first crises of the war. Pétain, the hero of Verdun, was a master of defensive warfare and a firm believer in wearing down the enemy with limited attacks, *'striking continually against the arch of the German structure until it collapses.'* In contrast, Foch, appointed Allied C-in-C in April 1918, remained the bristling spirit of the doctrine of all-out attack, although he was canny enough to sanction the use of a less expensive strategy in the summer of 1918.

Sir Douglas Haig, who succeeded French as the British C-in-C in December 1915, was a cool personality, virtually inarticulate at meetings, but a skilled political infighter with the ear of King George V. In recent years attempts have been made to rehabilitate Haig's reputation, but the fact remains that in 1916-17 his generalship cost the British Empire over 700,000 casualties to no discernible effect. His survival recalls the Tommys' melancholic dirge on the Western Front, *'We're 'ere because we're 'ere, because we're 'ere'.* Haig was there because he was there and no one better could be found to replace him.

Below: Haig and Foch in London in 1919. Foch, the dapper advocate of the offensive at all costs, and Haig, the monosyllabic political infighter, enjoyed a wary working relationship during Foch's time as Allied C-in-C in 1918.

REVOLUTION

BY EARLY 1917 Russia's disintegrating war machine, and the huge losses it had incurred supporting its allies, had brought it to the brink of collapse. To war-weariness was added starvation in Russia's cities.

In March food riots in Petrograd (St Petersburg) coalesced into a widespread uprising which forced the Tsar to abdicate. In July a charismatic socialist, Alexander Kerensky, became head of a Provisional government committed to continuing the war. However, effective power in Russia's cities lay with the Councils of Worker's and Soldier's Deputies – the Soviets.

The capture of Riga by the Germans on 1 September brought the Russian giant to its knees. Thousands of troops threw down their arms and walked home. They had *'voted with their feet'*, as it was put by the Bolshevik leader Lenin, who in April had returned to Russia with German connivance, in a sealed train.

Below: The beginning of the end. An anti-war demonstration in Petrograd in February 1917. In January 1917 an English nurse serving with the Russians wrote: 'Sabotage – railroads destroyed, workshops looted. Mobs shouting "Peace and Bread". They are aware the war is at the root of their hardships. The Tsar wishes to please everybody and pleases no one. We are amazed at newspaper criticisms of the government. A few months ago the writers would have been arrested. Things cannot continue as they are'.

Unlike the embattled Kerensky, Lenin had no interest in defeating Germany or making the world safe for democracy. When the vacillating Kerensky finally moved against the Bolsheviks at the beginning of November, their Red Guards seized the Winter Palace in Petrograd and arrested the Provisional Government. Now in power, the Bolsheviks opened peace talks with Germany in December in the bleak Polish fortress town of Brest Litovsk. German forces were within 100 miles of Petrograd when, on 3 March, the Russian delegates signed a peace treaty, giving up Poland, Lithuania, the Ukraine, the Baltic provinces and Transcaucasia. Germany then moved 40 divisions to the Western Front.

Left: Alexander Kerensky, who tried and failed to induce the Russians to continue the fight against the Germans.

Below: They voted with their feet. Soldiers walking home from the front as the Russian army crumbled away under the impact of the last great German offensive on the Eastern Front.

THE BIRTH OF THE BOMBER

BY MAY 1917 the German Army had become disillusioned with airships and had developed a bomber capable of raiding targets in Britain – the Gotha GIV. An attack on the port of Folkestone on 25 May 1917 was followed by two dramatic daylight raids on London on 13 June and 7 July.

The raids caused a huge furore about the state of Britain's air defences, the rapid improvement of which soon forced the Gothas to bomb by night. Meanwhile the British set about forming their own strategic bombing force, which emerged in the spring of 1918 as the fledgling RAF's Independent Force, based in France and given the task of attacking German war industry.

The Independent Force's main weapon was the Handley Page 0/400, which had a maximum bombload of 2,000lb. Bad weather and demands for their use in a tactical role in the final Allied offensives of the war meant that the 0/400s flew only a fraction of their missions against German war factories. As the war drew to a close, frantic efforts were made to bring the massive Handley Page V/500 into service to launch 'terror raids' on Berlin, but the huge biplane never flew in anger. Bombing did little or nothing to alter the course of the war, but in four years had nevertheless achieved a degree of sophistication undreamt of in 1914, when pilots had gaily lobbed grenades from the cockpits of their aircraft on to enemy formations below.

Below: A range of bombs displayed in front of a German Gotha GIV bomber, an aircraft earmarked for the raids on Britain. Its successor, the GV, had a maximum speed of of 87.5mph at 11,483ft, an operational ceiling of 21,325ft, range of 520 miles and 700-pound bombload on operations over southern England. An unusual feature of the GIV and GV was the gunner's 'sting in the tail'; he was provided with a wide ventral tunnel which allowed him to fire downwards and to the rear, much to the discomfiture of air defence fighters attacking from this quarter.

Above: The Handley page V/500, the largest British aircraft of World War I, built to bomb Berlin. Only three were delivered before the Armistice, and total production was 35 aircraft. The V/500 had a 126ft wingspan and was powered by four 375hp Rolls Royce engines mounted in tandem pairs midway between the wings. It could carry 30 250-pound bombs on short-range missions or a 1000-pound payload to Berlin. It never flew against Germany but a single machine was used in air control operations on India's Northwest Frontier in 1919.

Right: Aircrew of the Royal Naval Air Service demonstrate the methods used to attack the Zeppelin shed at Dusseldorf in September-October 1914, an early example of strategic bombing. The hand-dropped missiles are 20-pound Hale bombs. On 8 October the Zeppelin shed and the fully inflated airship inside were destroyed by a Sopwith Tabloid flown by Flight Lieutenant R.L.G. Marix.

NEW TACTICS TO BREAK THE DEADLOCK

TO OVERHAUL military doctrine in the middle of an all-out war is a daunting task, but in 1917 the German Army rose to the challenge.

In the winter of 1916-17 the German high command adopted the concept of 'elastic defence in depth' on the Western Front. Manpower was reduced in the front line, whose defensive positions were simultaneously strengthened and deepened. This enabled a more mobile defence and offered the possibility of the tactical surrender of territory. Special counter-attack divisions were held behind these new defensive positions, the so-called Hindenburg Line, to which the Germans retired in February-March 1917.

New infantry tactics were developed. Realizing that frontal attacks in extended lines were horribly wasteful of human lives, the Germans trained storm troopers to infiltrate

Below and Right: German storm troops in action on the Western Front in 1918. They were supported by rapid and accurate artillery fire loosed off in hurricane bombardments. They bypassed enemy strongpoints, leaving them to be mopped up in the infantry follow-up. Theses tactics were aimed at achieving deep penetration with mobility maintained by means of sled-hauled machine-guns, horse-drawn light artillery and lorry-mounted observation balloons to spot for artillery. The advance was co-ordinated by an elaborate series of light signals. The storm troopers were also equipped with the new Bergmann light machine-gun which had been introduced in 1917.

enemy lines behind a rolling barrage, bypassing strongpoints. These tactics, combined with the abandonment of a prolonged preliminary bombardment, proved successful on the Eastern Front in September 1917 during the capture of Riga by General Oskar von Hutier. They were employed in the German counter-offensive at Cambrai in the following November, and were to play a major part in the German spring offensive of 1918.

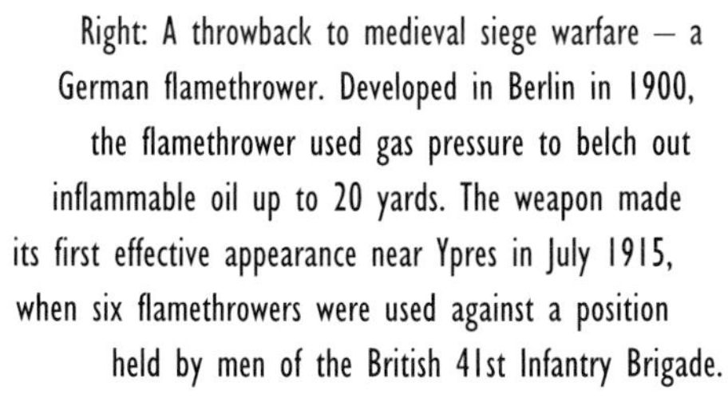

Right: A throwback to medieval siege warfare – a German flamethrower. Developed in Berlin in 1900, the flamethrower used gas pressure to belch out inflammable oil up to 20 yards. The weapon made its first effective appearance near Ypres in July 1915, when six flamethrowers were used against a position held by men of the British 41st Infantry Brigade.

LUDENDORFF'S LAST THROW 1

TOWARDS THE end of March 1918 the Germans launched what they hoped would be a knock-out blow in the West. As Ludendorff put it: '*The situation in Russia and Italy makes it possible to deliver a blow on the Western Front in the New Year. Our general situation requires that we should strike at the earliest possible moment before the Americans can throw strong forces in*'.

The German high command hoped to drive a wedge between the French and the British, the former concentrating on the defence of Paris, the latter casting anxious eyes over their shoulders to their communications with the Channel ports. The attack, spearheaded by storm troops using Hutier tactics, began in thick fog on 21 March. The British commander, Haig, had correctly anticipated the offensive but had deployed most of his reserves in the north, risking the security of the thinly spread British Fifth Army – against which the main German blow was aimed on the Somme – in order to insure against a less probable risk to the Channel ports.

Paris came under fire from long-range guns on 23 March. On 2 April, Haig had to submit to the appointment of the French Marshal Foch as the Allied Supreme Commander. A week later, with the first German thrust running out of steam and ammunition, Ludendorff launched a second blow against the British in Flanders. On 12 April Haig issued his famous 'backs to the wall' order, forbidding withdrawal.

Right: Storm troopers crash past a fallen Frenchman in March 1918. By the time of the last great German offensive the French had almost exhausted their manpower potential; 100 divisions on the Western Front had been reduced to infantry establishments of 6,000, half the 1914 figure. If anything the British were in an even worse plight.

Opposite below: British wounded are marched to the rear through the streets of Saint Quentin, March 1918, during the second Battle of the Somme. The impetus of the German advance was slowed considerably by the looting and indiscipline of the infantry.

Below: German infantry train for the Ludendorff offensive at Sedan in February 1918.

LUDENDORFF'S LAST THROW 2

LUDENDORFF'S second blow nearly broke the British, who were initially denied help by Foch. But by the end of April the Germans had been halted at a cost to the British Army of 239,793 casualties in 40 days of fighting. The Germans had lost close on 348,000 men, prompting Ludendorff to write that his troops *'thought with horror of fresh defensive fighting'.*

Now running out of cards, Ludendorff mounted an offensive against the French Sixth Army in Champagne. It began on 27 May when 17 divisions stormed the Chemin des Dames ridge in the Aisne sector. This was to be a diversion before the final blow fell on the British. The Germans broke through and by 3 June were once again on the Marne, near Château-Thierry, only 56 miles from Paris.

Here the Americans made a decisive intervention. General Pershing rushed the the US 3rd and 2nd Divisions into action on the Marne, while 50 miles to the northwest, at Cantigny, the US 1st Division was thrown into the US Army's first offensive action of the war. For three days the Americans blocked the German advance at Château-Thierry and then counter-attacked with the French in mid-June after the Germans had been fought to a halt.

Right: An order arrives by field telephone at an American artillery battery near Château-Thierry.

Below: Ever ready but seldom used. British cavalry resting near Montreuil, May 1918. The Western Front had reduced cavalry to an anachronism. At the Somme in 1916 and at Arras in 1917, German machine-guns had wrought havoc with cavalry when they were brought into the attack. Ironically the tonnage of fodder required to maintain the BEF's cavalry and transport animals exceeded that for ammunition; between 1914 and 1918 the horses ate their way through 5.9 million tons compared with the 5.2 million tons of shells and bullets which crossed the Channel.

Ludendorff then delivered a double blow east and west of Rheims, supported by a great weight of artillery. In the eastern sector the French had made a tactical withdrawal and the Germans found themselves punching thin air. To the west they crossed the Marne on a three-mile front but German exhaustion, and plans for a crushing French counterblow, were about to wrest the initiative away from the German high command.

Above: Men of the US First Division, the 'Big Red One', in action at Cantigny, which they took on 28 May, an indication that a new force had entered the field. Small as this and other American successes were compared with the overall picture, it meant that the writing was on the wall for the German High Command. It had lost the race against time.

THE BLACK DAY OF THE GERMAN ARMY

ON 24 July 1918, Foch assembled the three Allied Commanders-in-Chief – Haig, Pétain and Pershing – at his headquarters. He told them, *'The moment has come to abandon the general defensive attitude forced on us until now by numerical inferiority and pass to the offensive'.*

The blow fell on 8 August. Once more the British attacked on the Somme, but this time their preparations had been concealed from the Germans with the greatest skill. Learning the lessons of Cambrai, the British and French avoided a preliminary bombardment and supported the attack with 462 tanks. Fog masked the initial thrust, which within 24 hours had driven 10 miles into the German lines. Ludendorff wrote: *'8 August was the black day of the German Army in the history of war'.* The Germans fell back on the Hindenburg Line after suffering at least 100,000 casualties.

On 11 August Ludendorff tendered his resignation to the Kaiser, who refused it but nevertheless observed, *'I see that we must strike a balance. We have nearly reached the limit of our powers of resistance. The war must be ended'.*

Right: Seaforth Highlanders clear a German dugout, August 1918.

Below: The 13th Australian Light Horse move up to the front on 22 August during the clearing of the approaches to the Hindenburg Line. This operation cost the British 190,000 casualties between 8 August and 26 September 1918.

Above: The wreckage of war. All that was left of the great Cloth Hall at Ypres by September 1918.

ST MIHIEL

IN SPITE of the Kaiser's prophetic words, the war continued. The final assault on the Hindenburg Line began at the end of September after a preliminary American operation against the St Mihiel salient, which had threatened Allied movements in Champagne since 1914.

Foch, the Allied Supreme Commander, gave the task to Pershing's US First Army. It was the first independent action undertaken by the Americans in the war. The attack was launched against the two sides of the salient on 12 September, combined with an assault against the centre by French troops. The Germans were caught in the act of leisurely retirement from the salient, and were bundled out by the Americans in the space of 36 hours.

The clearing of the St Mihiel salient was followed by the decisive Allied offensive of the war, the centrepiece of which was the breaking of the Hindenburg Line with a drive by French and US troops along the Meuse valley towards Mézierès and a British thrust east of the Somme. By mid-October, after heavy fighting in which the Americans suffered severe losses in the Argonne forest, the German Army was on the point of disintegration.

Right: Infantry of the US First Army attack German positions in the St Mihiel salient in the first independent action undertaken by General Pershing.

Above: A klaxon warns of a gas attack on an American position. The Americans suffered 58,000 gas casualties, nearly half of them caused by mustard gas. Its effects did not become apparent for up to 12 hours. Then it began to rot the body within and without, causing blistering and vomiting and stripping off the mucous membrane in the bronchial tubes. It might take a month for a man to die, strapped to his bed in excrutiating agony.

Right: American machine-gunners in the Argonne, a rough, thickly wooded region in which the Germans had prepared a defensive zone 14 miles deep. The inexperienced Americans took heavy casualties in the Argonne before they broke out into open country at the beginning of November.

THE COLLAPSE OF GERMANY

BY THE beginning of October 1918, Germany's strategic position had been fatally undermined. One-by-one her allies had fallen by the wayside. On 25 September Bulgaria asked for peace. In Palestine, Turkish forces were in full retreat. In Italy the Austrian Army was on its last legs. On 27 October, Ludendorff resigned.

Inside Germany, hunger and a growing influenza epidemic were taking a heavy toll. In the port of Kiel 40,000 sailors mutinied. Austria and Turkey signed ceasefire agreements. On 9 November a socialist government seized power in Germany and the Kaiser abdicated. Since the night of 7 November a German delegation had been negotiating with Foch in his railway carriage headquarters at Compiègne. They had been instructed to sign whatever terms were offered. When they asked Foch what his terms for peace were, he replied *'None'.* The Germans admitted that they could not fight on. Foch replied, *'Then you have come to surrender'.*

At dawn on 11 November a message went out to all the Allied armies. The opening words were: *'Hostilities will cease at 11 hours today, November 11th'.* The guns were to fall silent. At first the men at the front could not come to terms with the quiet which lapped their positions. After over four years of war it was eerie not to hear gunfire somewhere. Relief came later, then jubilation.

Below: The face of defeat. German prisoners of war in 1918. At the time of the Armistice, on 11 November, the German Army remained unbroken but the political will to continue the war had evaporated.

Right: The meeting in a railway carriage where the Armistice was signed which ended the war. In June 1940, Adolf Hitler forced the defeated French to sign an armistice in the same carriage.

Left: Supporters of Germany's new socialist government near the Brandenburg Gate, Berlin, 9 November 1918.

AFTERMATH 1

IN THE summer of 1918 Germany occupied vast tracts of western Russia, containing one-third of her agricultural land and over half her industry. Through her Bulgarian and Austrian satellites, she controlled the Balkans. In the West, German armies were only 50 miles from Paris, having regained all the territory contested with France since the First Battle of the Marne in 1914.

Five months later the war had been won, not by the Germans but by the British, French and Americans. The German army, undefeated in the field and still numbering over 200 divisions, had effectively demobilized itself and marched home.

The feeling among Germans that they had been 'stabbed in the back' was increased when the victorious Allies met at Versailles in January 1919 to redraw the map of Europe, a task made all the more urgent by the collapse of the Russian, Austro-Hungarian and Ottoman empires.

Below: The Big Four at Versailles, Premier Orlando of Italy, David Lloyd George, the French Prime Minister Clemenceau and the US President Woodrow Wilson. In effect it was the Big Three as Orlando was confined to the sidelines of discussions, occasionally intervening to voice Italy's interests.

By the time of the Versailles conference a cloud of ambiguity hung over the Allied victory. The Allies themselves were now disarming. Although Germany was prostrate, and her very existence placed in doubt by revolution, her potential to rise again remained intact. To the French, above all, the securing of a durable peace meant the neutralization of Germany's potential by political or economic means. While the Germans considered the final terms, presented to them on 16 June, the Allies remained ready to resume war and the naval blockade on Germany stayed in place.

Below: British infantry raise their helmets to peace on 12 November 1918.

Below: The German fleet surrenders. The battleship *Friedrich der Grosse* sails into internment at the British naval base at Scapa Flow on 21 November 1918. The warships of the High Seas Fleet were later scuttled on the orders of their commanders.

AFTERMATH 2

THE TREATY was signed on 28 June. The numbers of the German armed forces and the arms they might bear were severely limited. Germany also lost all her colonies and much territory in Europe. France took Alsace-Lorraine, the Belgians Eupen and Malmédy, the Poles much of Posen and West Prussia. Danzig was to become a Free State and plebiscites were to decide the future of Upper Silesia, Schleswig and the Saar (which was first to have 15 years of international administration). The French were given control of the coal mines in the Saar to compensate for the German wrecking of their own mines in north-east France.

The east bank of the Rhine was demilitarized to a depth of 30 miles and occupied by the Allies for 15 years. The cost of this occupation was to be met by the Germans, who were also to make repayments for war damage to the tune of 6,600 million pounds sterling, a sum fixed by a Reparations Committee in 1921.

The treaty with Germany concluded the main business of the Versailles Conference, but work continued for the next 12 months on agreeing the boundaries of the states which were to emerge from the collapse of Austria-Hungary and the administration of large chunks of the Ottoman empire in the Middle East.

Below: The front page of London's Evening Standard tells the story of Armistice Day. An advertisement on the bottom right extols the virtues of a 'new custom of payment', by way of a cheque, which had become a commonplace transaction during the war years.

Fight INFLUENZA with BRAND'S ESSENCE OF BEEF
Of all Chemists and Stores

LATE NIGHT SPECIAL

Evening Standard

No. 29,428. LONDON, MONDAY, NOVEMBER 11, 1918. ONE PENNY.

Sell your Waste Paper to Lendrum's
HELP MUNITIONS AND THE NATION'S COMMERCE. LENDRUM Ltd., 3, Temple Avenue, London, E.C.4

END OF THE WAR

GERMANY SIGNS OUR TERMS & FIGHTING STOPPED AT 11 O'CLOCK TO-DAY.

ALLIES TRIUMPHANT.

FOCH AND LLOYD GEORGE TELL NEWS THAT SENT THE WORLD REJOICING.

BRITISH BACK AT MONS!

The following historic announcement, which means that the world war has come to an end at last, was issued by Mr. Lloyd George to the nation at 10.20 this morning:—

"THE ARMISTICE WAS SIGNED AT 5 a.m. THIS MORNING, AND HOSTILITIES ARE TO CEASE ON ALL FRONTS AT 11 a.m. TO-DAY."

The following message was sent out to-day through the wireless stations of the French Government.

"Marshal Foch to Commanders-in-Chief.

"Hostilities will cease on the whole front as from November 11th at 11 o'clock (French time).

"The Allied troops will not, until a further order, go beyond the line reached on that date and at that hour.

(Signed) MARSHAL FOCH.

The armistice negotiations opened on Friday morning, when the Germans were given until 11 a.m. to-day to accept or reject the Allied terms.

The signing of the terms of course means the end of the war, as the safeguards are such that it will be impossible for Germany to renew the struggle.

AT THE PALACE.

TERRIFIC OVATION FOR THE KING AND QUEEN.

Wonderful scenes of rejoicing were witnessed outside Buckingham Palace. As soon as the news became generally known in the West End thousands of people flocked towards Buckingham Palace, and cheered for a considerable time.

Hordes of children occupied the Victoria Statue, and the cheering was borne down the Mall. Soldiers passing on military motors joined in the glorification, people in taxicabs stood up and waved, and the Guards Band broke out into the strains of "Land of Hope and Glory." They had only got through the second verse when the music stopped, and from one of the main windows emerged the King and Queen, accompanied by Princess Mary and the Duke of Connaught. They faced the multitude from the balcony.

The appearance of the Royal party sent the crowd wild with enthusiasm. As the band played the National Anthem the King saluted solemnly, but when the strains of "Rule, Britannia," rang out his Majesty raised his naval cap and waved it enthusiastically. This led to a further demonstration on the part of the crowd.

Three thunderous cheers were given for Lloyd George, and immediately following considerable merriment was caused by the roar of an old seaman, "Poor old Tirps. We have finished his whiskers."

During the demonstration the Queen frequently waved her handkerchief in expression of her warm sympathy with the joy of the crowd.

Addressing from the balcony of the Palace the vast crowd, the King said:—

"With you I rejoice and thank God for the victories which the Allied armies have won and brought hostilities to an end and peace within sight."

When the guns commenced to fire there was renewed cheering and flag-wagging, while a party of munition girls formed themselves into a ring and danced and sang in joyous holiday mood.

At 12.20 the massed bands of the Guards assembled in the forecourt, and played the patriotic airs and other bright selections, to the great delight of the tremendous crowd assembled outside the Palace.

PEACE IN BRIEF.

BRITISH RECAPTURED MONS BEFORE THE FIGHTING STOPPED!

Armistice signed 5 a.m. to-day.

Hostilities ceased at 11 a.m.

British recaptured Mons this morning, and thus ended the war where our "Old Contemptibles" began it for us.

Erzberger evidently signed the armistice at Foch's G.H.Q. for the Germans.

German armies must evacuate to the east bank of the Rhine in 31 days.

London's lights are to go up to-night (full details on another page).

BACK TO THE RHINE.

One of the armistice terms is the withdrawal of the German armies to the east bank of the Rhine. The following table of distances will be of interest therefore:—

Towns.	Front.	Miles.
Ghent	Belgian	140
Mons	British	148
Maubeuge	British	155
Mezieres	French	162
Stenay	American	150
Alsace	American	20

ENVOYS RETURNING.

The German Plenipotentiaries are returning to Spa to-day.

THE ORDER OF GOING.

Armistices have been signed as follows:

Bulgaria	Sept. 29, 1918
Turkey	Oct. 30, 1918
Austria-Hungary	Nov. 3, 1918
Germany	Nov. 11, 1918

FULL ARMISTICE TERMS

EVACUATION TO THE RHINE AND BRIDGEHEADS FOR ALLIES.

U-BOATS TO SURRENDER.

GUNS HANDED OVER AND BATTLE SHIPS DISARMED.

REPATRIATING PRISONERS.

The terms of the armistice signed by the German plenipotentiaries were read in the House of Commons this afternoon by Mr. Lloyd George.

The armistice terms include evacuation of invaded territories, Belgium, France, Alsace-Lorraine, Luxembourg, to be completed within 14 days.

Railways of Alsace-Lorraine to be handed over.

German troops who have not left these territories within 14 days to be treated as prisoners of war. The occupation by the Allied and United States forces will keep pace with the evacuation.

The evacuation by the enemy of Rhine lands must be completed within 16 days.

Immediate repatriation without reciprocity of Allied and United States prisoners.

All German troops in Russia, Rumania, and elsewhere to be withdrawn. Complete abandonment of the treaties of Bukharest and Brest-Litovsk.

Immediate cessation of all hostilities at sea. Handing over to Allies and United States of all submarines.

The surrender by the German Government of the following equipment:— 5000 guns, of which 2500 will be heavy and 2500 field guns, 30,000 machine-guns, and a large number of trench-mortars.

Six battle cruisers, ten battleships, eight light cruisers, 50 destroyers, and other services are to be disarmed, and the Allies reserve the right to occupy Heligoland to enable them to enforce the terms of the armistice.

BREST-LITOVSK TREATY ABANDONED.

By Our Parliamentary Representatives.

HOUSE OF COMMONS, Monday.

There are large crowds in Palace Yard outside the Houses of Parliament. Mr. Lloyd George arrived in a motorcar, accompanied by Mrs. Lloyd George and Mr. Bonar Law, Sir Eric Geddes following behind in another motorcar. The two cars were preceded by a mounted policeman, who made a way through the cheering crowds.

When the Prime Minister entered the House he was greeted by his colleagues with tumultuous cheering. Immediately at the conclusion of prayers the Prime Minister was called upon by the Speaker.

Mr. Lloyd George said: The armistice, as has already been announced in the Press, was signed this morning at 5 o'clock, after a discussion which was prolonged all night. I will read to the House of Commons the conditions of the armistice, in so far as they have reached me up to the present.

I have to warn the House and the public that we only received such corrections as were rendered necessary by the new conditions by telephone, and there is a possibility that there may be a few mistakes, but substantially this represents the conditions which Germany has accepted.

CLAUSES RELATING TO THE WESTERN FRONT.

Cessation of hostilities by land and in the air six hours after the signature of the armistice.

Mr. Lloyd George remarked that the armistice was signed at 5 o'clock in the morning, and the war ceased at 11 o'clock this morning.

Immediate evacuation of invaded territories,

(Continued on Page 8.)

The 1914-18 conflict had ostensibly been the war fought to end all wars. The instrument by which new wars were to be prevented and peace maintained was the League of Nations, the formation of which had been the last of President Wilson's famous 'Fourteen Points' for peace. From the start, however, the League was hamstrung by the United States' refusal to join it. Marshal Foch, the Allied Supreme Commander in 1918, remained convinced that Germany would rise again. He boycotted the signing of the Versailles Treaty, observing with some accuracy that *'This is not peace. It is an armistice for 20 years'.*

Below: The debris of war: A pile of German steel helmets await destruction.

Below: Armistice Day celebrations in London, 11 November 1918. Winston Churchill remembered: '. . . I looked into the street. It was deserted. Then from all sides men and women came into the street. The bells began to clash. Thousands rushing in a frantic manner, shouting, screaming. Flags appeared. . . London streets were in pandemonium'.

COUNTING THE COST

IT IS impossible to estimate the final human cost of the war. The Russians suffered the most, losing as many as 3* million dead before the ravages of famine and civil war took their toll. The Austro-Hungarian empire lost at least 1.2 million dead and 3.6 million wounded, but these incomplete returns are almost certainly an underestimate. German figures are also uncertain; their own estimate was that they had suffered nearly 1.9 million dead and 4.3 million wounded. The French had total casualties of 5 million of which 1.4 million were dead or missing. The British empire suffered 3.2 million casualties of whom nearly a million were dead or missing. Of these some 745,000 came from the United Kingdom. Fighting on a narrow single front (with the exception of small contingents in Salonika and France) the Italians lost 460,000 dead. It is worth noting that this figure represents almost exactly half of the death toll of the entire British empire on all fronts. The Turks estimated their losses at 2.3 million, while the United States sustained 326,000 casualties, of whom nearly 116,000 were dead, 206,000 wounded and 4,500 prisoners or missing.

Below: The road to Chepilly strewn with men killed in the fighting of August 1918. The American poet Ezra Pound wrote an epitaph for them, and for those who survived:

'Died, some pro patria,
non "dulce" non "et decor" . . .
Walked eye deep in hell
believing in old men's lies,
then unbelieving
came home, home to a lie,
home to many deceits,
home to old lies and new infamy'.

*Figures quoted in *The First World War* by John Terraine (Leo Cooper, 1983).

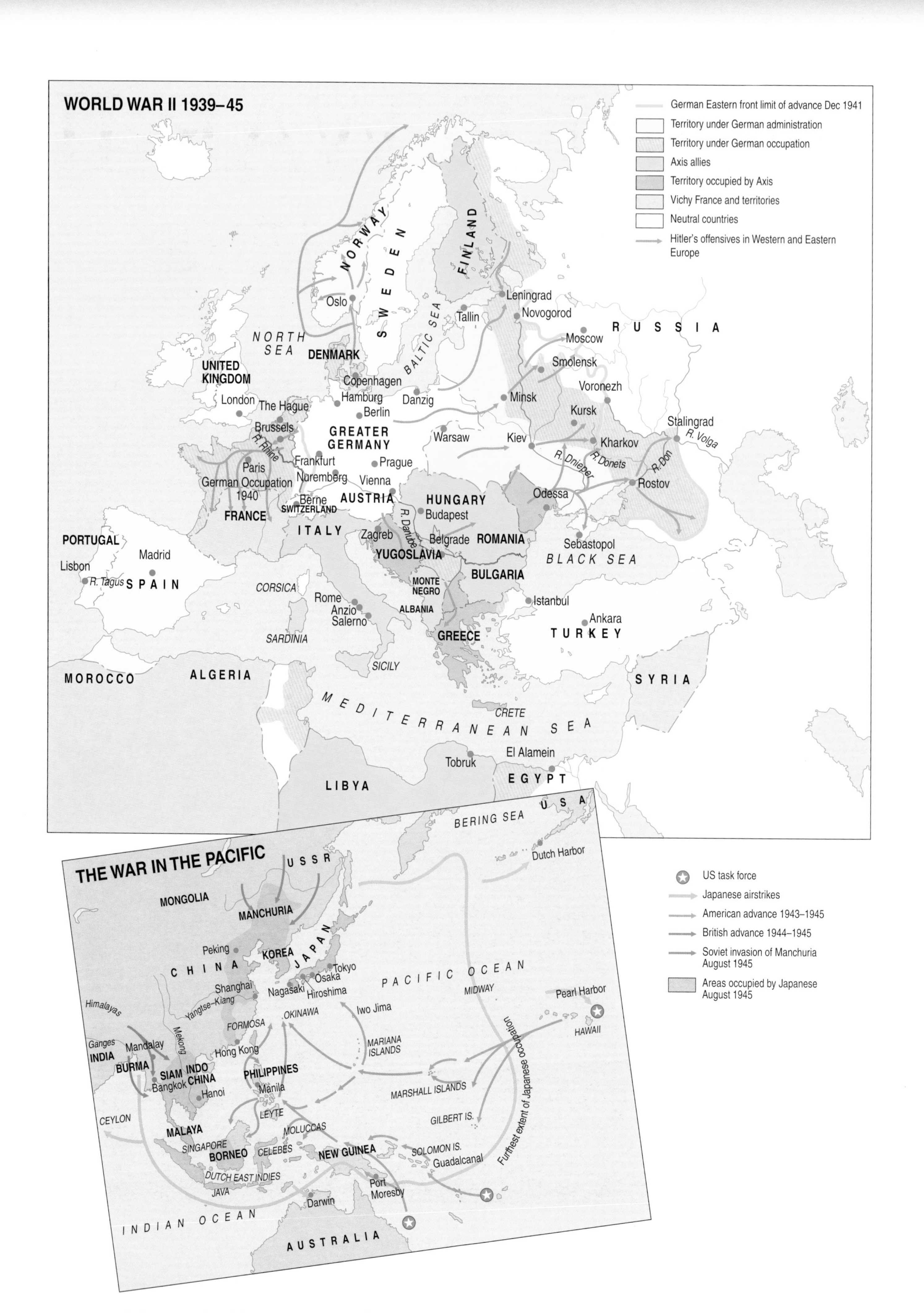

WORLD WAR II 1939–45
German Eastern front limit of advance Dec 1941
Territory under German administration
Territory under German occupation
Axis allies
Territory occupied by Axis
Vichy France and territories
Neutral countries
Hitler's offensives in Western and Eastern Europe
NORWAY
SWEDEN
FINLAND
Oslo
Leningrad
Novogorod
Tallin
BALTIC SEA
NORTH SEA
DENMARK
RUSSIA
Moscow
Smolensk
UNITED KINGDOM
Copenhagen
Hamburg
Danzig
Minsk
Voronezh
London
The Hague
Berlin
Kursk
Stalingrad
R. Volga
Brussels
R. Rhine
GREATER GERMANY
Warsaw
Kiev
Kharkov
Paris
Frankfurt
Prague
R. Dnieper
R. Donets
R. Don
German Occupation 1940
Nuremberg
Vienna
Rostov
Odessa
Berne
SWITZERLAND
AUSTRIA
HUNGARY
Budapest
FRANCE
ITALY
Zagreb
R. Danube
Belgrade
ROMANIA
Sebastopol
PORTUGAL
YUGOSLAVIA
BLACK SEA
Madrid
Lisbon
R. Tagus
SPAIN
CORSICA
MONTE NEGRO
BULGARIA
Istanbul
Rome
Anzio
Salerno
ALBANIA
Ankara
SARDINIA
GREECE
TURKEY
SICILY
MOROCCO
ALGERIA
SYRIA
MEDITERRANEAN SEA
CRETE
El Alamein
Tobruk
LIBYA
EGYPT
THE WAR IN THE PACIFIC
BERING SEA
USA
USSR
Dutch Harbor
MONGOLIA
MANCHURIA
Peking
KOREA
JAPAN
Tokyo
CHINA
Osaka
Shanghai
Nagasaki
Hiroshima
PACIFIC OCEAN
MIDWAY
Pearl Harbor
HAWAII
Himalayas
Yangtse-Kiang
OKINAWA
Iwo Jima
FORMOSA
MARIANA ISLANDS
Furthest extent of Japanese occupation
Ganges
INDIA
Mandalay
Mekong
Hong Kong
BURMA
SIAM
INDO CHINA
PHILIPPINES
Bangkok
Manila
Hanoi
MARSHALL ISLANDS
CEYLON
LEYTE
GILBERT IS.
MALAYA
MOLUCCAS
SINGAPORE
BORNEO
CELEBES
NEW GUINEA
SOLOMON IS.
Guadalcanal
DUTCH EAST INDIES
JAVA
Port Moresby
Darwin
INDIAN OCEAN
AUSTRALIA
US task force
Japanese airstrikes
American advance 1943–1945
British advance 1944–1945
Soviet invasion of Manchuria August 1945
Areas occupied by Japanese August 1945

WORLD WAR II

IN PHOTOGRAPHS

Flag raising on Iwo Jima, February 23 1945.

THE ROAD TO WAR 1

THE SECOND World War was the last great battle of the war of 1914-18. The manner of Germany's defeat in 1918, with its army still in the field, and the reparations and territorial losses imposed by the Treaty of Versailles, left a permanent legacy of bitterness. Agitators like the ex-soldier Adolf Hitler, leader of the nascent Nazi Party, fed on these feelings of betrayal. Hitler's opinion of the Versailles settlement was simple: *'Only fools, liars and criminals could hope for mercy from the enemy . . . hatred grew in me, hatred for those responsible for the dead.'* His political career was to be devoted to the overturning of the Treaty of Versailles and the restoration of Germany as a world power.

After the failure of his Munich putsch in November 1923 and subsequent imprisonment, Hitler pursued a constitutional path to power, becoming German Chancellor in January 1933. A year later he announced that henceforth he would be German Head of State and Commander-in-Chief of the armed forces, binding them to him with an oath of allegiance.

Below: A disabled veteran of the trenches begs in a Berlin street in 1923, the year in which Adolf Hitler launched his unsuccessful coup in Munich. In the immediate postwar years Germany was wracked by bitter disillusion, raging inflation and pitched street battles between the private armies of the Communists and the extreme right.

The impressive German economic recovery of the 1930s – achieved by a bold policy of deficit financing – underwrote Hitler's policy of rearmament, at first undertaken secretly and then announced to the world on 16 March 1935. Skilful propaganda concealed the underlying weakness of Germany's rapidly expanding armed forces, and their strength was constantly overestimated abroad.

Below: A truck full of troops trundles through Berlin's Potsdamer Platz during the Kapp putsch of March 1920. This attempt to seize power from Germany's Weimar Republic was supported by a significant section of the Army. It was during this period of chronic political and economic instability that Adolf Hitler emerged as the leader of the National Socialist German Workers' Party – the Nazi Party.

Right: The eyes have it. Adolf Hitler, ill at ease in a lounge suit, hones his spellbinding style with the help of his personal photographer Heinrich Hoffman, an earthy Bavarian who became the unofficial jester at the Nazi court.

THE ROAD TO WAR 2

WAR, OR rather the threat of it, was the driving force behind Hitler's foreign policy in the 1930s. He played brilliantly on the popular desire for peace in France and Britain, their governments' fear of a bloodletting even more terrible than that of 1914-18, and their inability to ally with the Soviet Union.

In March 1936 he reoccupied the demilitarized Rhineland, against the advice of his senior commanders. Britain and France failed to react, and Hitler embarked on an increasingly aggressive foreign policy. 'Volunteers' and much material went to General Franco's Nationalist forces in Spain for combat testing in the Spanish Civil War. In March 1938 Hitler annexed Austria. Czechoslovakia was next on his list. In September 1938 he outmanoeuvred the British and French at Godesberg and Munich to seize control of the Sudetenland and its ethnic German population. In March 1939 he swallowed up the rest of Czechoslovakia.

Below: The entry of the colours at the annual Nazi Party rally at Nuremberg, held every year in September. The Rally combined impressive demonstrations of growing German military might with the acutely skilful manipulation of mass emotion. In the vast perspectives of the Nuremberg stadium, which hosted the 1936 Olympic Games, thousands of perfectly drilled formations, flypasts of warplanes, torchlit processions and domed searchlights conveyed an overwhelming impression of national power, unity and purpose.

Left: Be prepared. A nightmarish vision of the future in which British Post Office workers take part in a 1937 anti-gas exercise. During the crisis over Czechoslovakia in 1938, 38 million gas mask were issued to men, women and children in Britain. In the late 1930s fears about the use of gas were justified. In 1935 The Italian dictator Benito Mussolini had used chemical weapons in his conquest of Ethiopia.

In the same month the Lithuanian port of Memel, with its large German population, was ceded to Germany. Hitler then turned to the free port of Danzig and the Polish Corridor to the Baltic, which separated East Prussia from Germany proper. On 23 August he secured his eastern flank by signing a non-aggression pact with the Soviet Union. War was now only a few days away.

Right: The first of the few. The Royal Air Force's 19 Squadron shows off its new Supermarine Spitfire fighters in the summer of 1938. In the autumn of that year the RAF's Fighter Command mustered 573 obsolete biplanes and only 93 monoplane aircraft. By then the German air force, the Luftwaffe, had used the Spanish Civil War to combat test its new Me109 fighter, He111 bomber and Ju87 dive-bomber.

THE INVASION OF POLAND

BEFORE DAWN on 1 September the German air force, the Luftwaffe, began a bombardment of strategic points inside Poland. It was the prelude to the first full-scale demonstration of the speed and striking power of *Blitzkrieg* (Lightning War) tactics, developed in the 1930s and based on deep armoured thrusts supported by dive- and level-bombers.

The Polish army was dispersed in seven concentrations along its borders, with little in reserve, inviting swift envelopment by the German Army Group South, attacking on Poland's western frontier, and Army Group North, striking south from Pomerania and East Prussia.

Within two days the Luftwaffe had gained complete control of the air and the Polish cordon defences were splintered into unco-ordinated groups. The German plan involved a double pincer movement. The inner pincer (Fourth, Eighth and Tenth Armies) was to close on the Vistula near Warsaw, while the outer pincer (Third and Fourteenth Armies) was to meet on the River Bug at Brest Litovsk, 100 miles east of the Polish capital.

STEPS TO WAR

20 August: Polish Crisis breaks.

23 August: Britain warns Germany that she will fulfil her guarantees to Poland if Poland is attacked. German-Soviet Non-Aggression Pact signed in Moscow. Secret protocol agrees to partition of Poland and Soviet occupation of Baltic states.

24 August: British Parliament approves Emergency Powers Bill.

25 August: Britain and Poland sign mutual assistance treaty.

31 August: Hitler orders attack on Poland.

2 September: Poland's allies Britain and France issue ultimatum to Germany.

3 September: Britain and France declare war on Germany after ultimatum is ignored.

Above right: Day of the dive-bomber. Junkers Ju87 'Stukas' over Poland. Roaming at will over the battlefield, the Stukas played.havoc with Polish infantry and cavalry columns. The aircraft's fearsome reputation as a battle-winner belied its relatively modest performance, with a top speed of about 260mph and a bombload of 1,100 pounds.

Right: Hitler takes the salute as the victorious German Army marches through the streets of Warsaw. The long Polish nightmare was about to begin. It was the German aim not merely to dominate the Poles but totally to destroy their national identity. Poland was to become a slave nation.

Above: Forcing the frontier. German troops dismantle a barrier on the Polish border on 1 September 1939. At dawn that day the first of about a million men – concentrated in 41 infantry and 14 armoured (panzer) divisions – began to pour into Poland. The Poles fielded as many infantry but had little armour.

The outer encirclement was completed on 14 September. Three days later Poland's fate was sealed when the Red Army invaded from the east. Warsaw surrendered on the 27th and the fortress city of Modlin fell on the following day. The last Polish resistance was overcome at Kock, south-east of Warsaw, on 5 October. Polish casualties totalled 66,000 dead, over 200,000 wounded and nearly 700,000 prisoners. German casualties were light – some 10,500 dead, and 30,300 wounded.

THE PHONEY WAR

THE SPEED of German operations in Poland had, in part, been prompted by Hitler's fear that the French might launch an offensive in the West. In the event, the French and their British allies obliged him by remaining wholly inert.

The 150,000 troops of the British Expeditionary Force (BEF) which had crossed to France, dug in on the Belgian border but saw no action. Visiting the front line, Prime Minister Neville Chamberlain asked querulously, *'The Germans don't want to attack, do they?'* The greater part of the French Army, some 43 divisions, sat passively in or behind the Maginot Line, the fortress system on its eastern frontier. In September they made a feeble demonstration in the Saar, advanced a few miles, occupied a few abandoned villages and then withdrew.

There was an air of unreality about the war. The Royal Air Force was dropping propaganda leaflets rather than bombs on Germany. The bitter winter weather of 1939-40 was a greater threat to aircrew than the enemy's air defences. In Britain the 'Phoney War', as it came to be known, seemed to be a conflict run by civil servants rather than soldiers. The sole beneficiary was Adolf Hitler. Untroubled by the blockade on which the Allies pinned their hopes, he regrouped after the victory in Poland and planned his spring offensive, which was to begin with the invasion of Norway and Denmark.

Left: The shield of France. One of the huge guns in the Maginot Line, the embodiment in steel and concrete of the trench systems of World War I. Named after the French war minister who initiated it, the Maginot Line was meant to deter aggression but spoke volumes for the defensive mentality of the French Army. The Line's fatal weakness was that it could be outflanked through neutral Belgium.

Left: Scramble! Pilots of the RAF's 87 Squadron, part of the British Expeditionary Force in France, race for their Hurricanes in March 1940. At the time of its introduction into service in the autumn of 1937 the Hawker Hurricane was the first operational fighter capable of exceeding 300mph and the first to be armed with eight machine guns.

Above: Dominoes and gas masks in a London family's Anderson shelter. A corrugated iron construction sunk into thousands of back gardens, the Anderson shelter was to save many lives during the Blitz. It was named after Sir John Anderson, the British Home Secretary, 1939-40, a firm advocate of its use. Remembering nights in the Anderson shelter, the historian Norman Longmate wrote, 'To be inside an Anderson shelter felt rather like being entombed in a small, dark bicycle shed, smelling of earth and damp'.

Right: End of an ocean raider. The German pocket battleship *Graf Spee* ablaze in the River Plate off Montevideo, Uruguay, where she had taken refuge after a running battle with a British cruiser squadron. Rather than expose her to destruction by the heavier Royal Navy units steaming towards the Plate, Hitler ordered *Graf Spee* to be scuttled on 17 December 1939. Three days later her commander, Captain Hans Langsdorff, committed suicide.

THE TRIUMPH OF BLITZKRIEG

NORWAY WAS of strategic importance to Hitler as a springboard for aerial attack against Britain, and against the British naval blockade which threatened the route taken by the ships bringing Germany vital iron-ore from Sweden through the port of Narvik in northern Norway.

On 4 April 1940, Neville Chamberlain confidently announced that *'Hitler has missed the bus'*. Four days later British warships encountered German vessels escorting troop transports towards the Norwegian ports of Kristiansand, Stavanger, Bergen, Trondheim and Narvik. Far from missing the bus, Hitler was invading Norway.

Below: Bombs fall on the Norwegian port of Narvik. The Germans occupied the town on 9 April 1940. A week later the British and French landed a force in the area but Narvik did not fall to the Allies until the end of May. In two naval battles fought off Narvik in April, the Royal Navy destroyed half the complement of the German Navy's destroyers. Shortage of destroyers was to play a significant part in forestalling the German invasion of southern England in the summer of 1940.

Above: German infantry advance behind armoured cover through a clutter of bicycles. The skies above them were dominated by the Luftwaffe, which made life for the Allied troops extremely uncomfortable.

Right: The occupiers arrive. German troops disembark in Oslo in May 1940. In April the former war minister, Vidkun Quisling, whose name later became synonymous with treachery, proclaimed himself premier of a pro-German government, but real power lay with the German Reich Commissioner, Josef Terboven, who reported directly to Hitler. Norway's legitimate government and King Haakon VII had fled to London.

Only at Oslo, the Norwegian capital, did the Germans encounter serious resistance. The cruiser *Blücher* was sunk and the battleship *Lutzow* damaged before airborne troops captured the city. Denmark was overrun on 9 April.

Between 10 and 13 April the Royal Navy inflicted heavy damage on the German naval force ferrying troops to Narvik, and five days later the Allies landed near Narvik. Over the next three days they also landed north and south of Trondheim, but these footholds were eliminated by the Germans as they swept inland, and evacuations followed at the beginning of May. An Allied force captured Narvik on 28 May but was also forced to evacuate on June 8-9 because of events in France. In the withdrawal the carrier *Glorious* was sunk and the German battlecruisers *Scharnhorst* and *Gneisenau* were badly damaged.

THE FALL OF FRANCE

ON 10 MAY, the day Winston Churchill became British Prime Minister, Germany attacked Holland and Belgium, catching the British and French deployed in three army groups behind the French frontier.

The British and French high commands had expected the major German thrust to be directed through the Low Countries, as it had been in 1914, and indeed this was the original German intention. But the plan had been changed, and maximum pressure was now applied not in the north but through the heavily wooded Ardennes, which the Allies had thought impenetrable by tanks. France's supposedly impregnable Maginot Line was simply outflanked.

By 14 May, German tanks had crossed the Meuse at Sedan and were sweeping north to trap huge numbers of French and British troops in northern France and Belgium. German armour reached the English Channel on the 20th, and a week later the BEF, which had fallen back on the Channel ports, began its evacuations from Dunkirk. When Operation Dynamo ended on 4 June, some 338,000 troops (225,000 of them British) had been taken off the beaches. The next day the Germans began mopping up remaining French resistance. An armistice was signed on the 22nd, and four days later fighting ceased. Italy had declared war on Britain and France on 10 June.

Right: A Ju87 of the crack 'Immelmann' wing is prepared for take-off. Although the Stuka terrorized raw French troops during the Battle of France, its weaknesses were also exposed, notably its vulnerability when pulling out of a steep dive. It was withdrawn from the Battle of Britain in mid-August 1940, after suffering heavy losses at the hands of Fighter Command. Later in the war the Stuka was adapted to an anti-shipping role and performed sterling service on the Eastern Front as a heavily armed 'tank-buster'.

Left: British infantry under attack from the air as they await evacuation from the Dunkirk pocket. The destruction of the trapped Allied troops had been entrusted to the Luftwaffe by Hitler, who was preoccupied with the elimination of the remaining French armies south of the Somme and still fearful of an Allied counterstroke against his armour in an area cut by canals and threatend with flooding. The Luftwaffe failed in its task. In furious air battles over Dunkirk it lost 156 aircraft and the RAF 106.

Above: No other tourist has paid his first visit to Paris as a conqueror. Hitler inspects the Eiffel Tower at the end of June 1940. Walking on his right is the architect Albert Speer, who in 1942 became Hitler's highly capable Armaments Minister.

THE BATTLE OF BRITAIN

THE FALL of France had brought the seemingly invincible German army to the coast of France. Adolf Hitler brooded over the invasion of southern England, codenamed *Sealion*, an operation for which neither he nor his high command had any real enthusiasm.

The success of *Sealion* depended on the destruction by the Luftwaffe of the Royal Air Force's Fighter Command. The air battle began in earnest on 10 July 1940, and for three weeks the Luftwaffe and Fighter Command exchanged opening blows, probing each other's strengths and weaknesses.

Below: Ready to roll. A Messerschmitt Me 109 fighter of I/JG2 Richthofen taxis for take-off. The Me109 and the Spifire were evenly matched but the former was hampered by its combat range of 125 miles, which limited it to a maximum of 30 minutes over southern England. A Luftwaffe commander later complained: 'The German fighters found themselves in a similar predicament to a dog on a chain which wants to attack a foe but cannot harm him because of his limited orbit'.

The battle moved into a higher gear in August, and on 15 August the Luftwaffe launched its main attack, codenamed *Adler* (Eagle), to provoke and win a decisive battle against Fighter Command. In fierce air fighting the Luftwaffe lost 72 aircraft on what became known as 'Black Thursday'.

RAF losses, which were now outstripping the supply of new aircraft, were also causing concern. Exhaustion had set in among the battered squadrons defending the key battleground over south-east England. Several of Fighter Command's vital sector stations lay in ruins, although they were still flying off aircraft.

Throughout the battle, the Luftwaffe had fatally switched back and forth between targets – the RAF's coastal radar installations, Fighter Command's sector stations, aircraft factories – without knocking out any of them. On 7 September it launched its first mass daylight raid on London. The Luftwaffe believed that the RAF had only 100 aircraft left, but on 15 September it suffered a crushing defeat when two heavily escorted waves of bombers ran into nearly 300 British fighters in the skies over London. Air superiority had been decisively denied to the Luftwaffe, and on 12 October Hitler ordered the indefinite postponement of *Sealion*.

Right: Two Hurricanes of 501 Squadron scramble from Gravesend on 15 August at the height of the battle. Although less glamorous than the legendary Spitfire, the rugged Hurricane bore the brunt of the fighting in the Battle of Britain from July to November 1940. The top-scoring Fighter Command squadron of the Battle, 303, flew Hurricanes and is credited with 126½ confirmed victories.

Above: An armourer, one of the many unsung heroes of the Battle of Britain, readies a Spitfire for combat. Each aircraft had a ground crew of three – a rigger, fitter and armourer. The squadrons of Fighter Command were sustained by a long chain stretching back from the ground crews to the workers in aircraft factories.

Below: Luftwaffe aircrew are marched away from the burning wreckage of their He111. The speed of the twin-engined He111 was no guarantee of safety from Spitfires and Hurricanes, and a feature of the Battle of Britain was the high proportion of bombers which returned to their bases with dead and severely wounded crew.

THE BLITZ

ON SATURDAY 7 September 1940 the Luftwaffe launched its first attack on London. That afternoon its commander-in-chief, Reichsmarschall Hermann Göring, stood on the clifftop at Cap Gris Nez watching flights of bombers thundering overhead across the Channel. The Blitz was about to begin.

That day 300 aircraft dropped more than 300 tons of bombs on London's docks and the densely packed streets of the East End. The fires they started lit the way for 250 more bombers which attacked between 8pm and dawn. To a fire officer battling the blaze in the Surrey docks it seemed that *'the whole bloody world's on fire!'*

For the next 56 nights London was bombed from dusk to dawn, the bombers following the silver line of the Thames to strike at the biggest target in the world. By the end of the year the death toll in London had reached 13,600, with many thousands more injured and over 250,000 people left homeless. The cost to the Luftwaffe was negligible; anti-aircraft guns were downing only one enemy aircraft in every 300.

In the 1930s British planners calculated that civilian morale would crack almost as soon as the bombs started to fall. But as the weeks passed, people found that life was bearable in spite of the bombs. London proved too tough a nut to crack, and the Luftwaffe turned its attention to ports like Southampton and industrial centres in the Midlands. On 14 November the city of Coventry suffered a devastating raid which introduced a new word to the language – to 'Coventrate'.

The final phase of the Blitz began on 16 April 1941, climaxing with a huge raid on London on 10 May which left one-third of the capital's streets impassable and 160,000 families without water, gas and electricity. But by the end of June 1941 two-thirds of the Luftwaffe had been transferred to the Eastern Front. The Blitz was over.

Above: A Heinkel He111 drones over the East End of London. This dramatic photograph was distributed in Germany to suggest how vulnerable the capital of the British Empire was to Hitler's bombers. But by switching the attack to London on 8 September, partly in response to an RAF bombing raid on Berlin, Hitler threw away all chance of winning the Battle of Britain.

Right: A tin-hatted Air Raid Warden takes tea in his post, the lynchpin at a local level of Britain's civil defence system. Each post was supposed to control an area containing about 500 people. In London there were about ten posts a square mile. In 1939 there were 1.5 million civil defence personnel, over two-thirds of them volunteers.

Left: Spirit of the Blitz. In April 1941 Winston Churchill declared: 'I see the damage done by the enemy attacks; but I also see, side by side with the devastation and the ruins, quiet, confident, bright and smiling eyes, beaming with the consciousness of being associated with a cause far higher and wider than any human or personal issue. I can see the spirit of an unquenchable people'.

Right: Londoners take refuge from the bombs on the platform of the Elephant and Castle Underground station. At the height of the Blitz about 170,000 people sheltered in the Tube every night. Legend has it that their snoring rose and fell like a wind.

BALKAN INTERLUDE

SMARTING AT Hitler's success in the West, the Italian dictator Benito Mussolini invaded Albania and Greece in October 1940. He soon ran into trouble, was driven back into Albania by the Greeks and had to be rescued by his German ally.

Hitler also wanted to protect his southern flank before launching the long-planned invasion of the Soviet Union. When the pro-German Prince Paul of Yugoslavia was overthrown in a coup encouraged by the movement of 60,000 British troops to Greece, Hitler went on the offensive.

In Operation Punishment, which began on 6 April 1941, the Germans overran Yugoslavia in only ten days. The conquest of Greece took just over two weeks. The British evacuated some 18,000 of the troops in Greece to the island of Crete, which was captured by the Germans at the end of May after an airborne invasion. Nine British warships were sunk and 17 seriously damaged in a second evacuation.

The German victory in Crete was gained at the cost of nearly 10,000 casualties. Horrified at the losses, Hitler cancelled a proposed airborne seizure of Malta.

Right: The swastika is run aloft on the Parthenon in Athens. The campaigns in Greece and Yugoslavia cost the German Army barely 5,000 casualties. In Yugoslavia the Germans took 345,000 prisoners. Greek losses amounted to 70,000 killed or wounded and 270,000 captured. The British sustained 12,000 casualties in the Greek campaign and lost all their heavy equipment.

Right: A German transport aircraft goes down as parachutes fill the skies over north-west Crete on 20 May 1941. In the desperate fighting which followed the drops, the paratroops suffered heavy casualties, but their seizure of Maleme airfield gave them a foothold for airborne reinforcement which ensured victory.

Below: The British warship *Kipling* steams into Alexandria harbour after the fall of Crete. Waving to the shore from the bridge is the flamboyant Lord Mountbatten, commander of the Fifth Destroyer Flotilla, whose ship, the destroyer *Kelly*, had been sunk by Stukas during the British evacuation. Mountbatten and the survivors from *Kelly* were picked up by *Kipling*, which was also attacked and damaged by German aircraft. Mountbatten was later appointed Chief of Combined Operations before becoming Supreme Allied Commander, South-East Asia.

BARBAROSSA 1

AT 3.30am on Sunday 22 June 1941, the day after the 129th anniversary of Napoleon's attack on Russia in 1812, seven German infantry armies, their advance spearheaded by four panzer groups, invaded the Soviet Union. The codename for the operation was Barbarossa.

Three million German soldiers, supported by 3,580 tanks, 7,184 guns and nearly 2,000 aircraft were on the move along a front of 2,000 miles. The Red Army, in the middle of a wholesale reorganization and deployed forward to cover every curve and crevice in its frontiers, was caught in a series of massive encirclements. At Minsk and Smolensk in July, the Germans took 400,000 prisoners. In September, 600,000 went into the bag, trapped in the wide bend of the Dnieper.

Below: Armoured drive. A MkIII panzer and panzer grenadiers advance across a cornfield in the fierce heat of the Russian summer. The MkIII was the backbone of the panzer divisions in the early stages of the German campaign in Russia, but was to meet its match in the Russian T-34, the best all-round tank of the war, which was introduced in 1941.

Two months of victory exacted their price. Battle deaths, wounds and sickness struck half a million men from the German order of battle. On 11 July the commander of 18th Panzer Division expressed fears that the loss of men and equipment would prove insupportable *'if we do not intend to win ourselves to death'.*

Right: House to house fighting in Rostov, a major rail junction in southern Russia close to the Sea of Azov. The city fell to the German First Panzer Army on 21 November 1941, but was retaken by the Russians a week later after a fierce counterattack. It was the first serious setback for the Germans in Barbarossa and led to the resignation of the commander of Army Group South, Field Marshal von Rundstedt.

Below: A column of refugees in the Ukraine, with the smoke of battle rising behind them. Often described as the granary of Russia, the Ukraine was the objective of Army Group South in Barbarossa.

BARBAROSSA 2

EARLY IN October 1941 the depleted German Army Group North laid siege to Leningrad. But by now Russia's vast spaces, primitive roads and gruelling climate were taking their toll on the German Army.

Scorching summer heat gave way to seas of autumn mud. In October the first snows of winter began to fall. Hitler was now caught between driving straight for Moscow or reinforcing his extended southern flank to secure the raw materials and agricultural riches of the Ukraine. Winter – for which the German high command had not equipped its army – arrived while the Führer was still shuttling forces up and down his battlefront.

Below: The people of Moscow dig anti-tank ditches on the approaches to the Russian capital in the atumn of 1941. The setbacks of the opening phase of Barbarossa encouraged the Soviet dictator, Josef Stalin, to transform the struggle against Germany into the 'Great Patriotic War'. The Orthodox Church was enlisted in the war effort and 'Mother Russia' rather than the Communist Party invoked as a rallying cry.

Right: German motor transport trapped in the glutinous mud of the 1942 spring thaw. Russian winter cold was a quick killer but the endless seas of autumn and spring mud destroyed mobility and sapped morale. On Russia's primitive roads twelve hours of rain was enough to reduce a main highway to an impassable morass. In these conditions, horsed transport came into its own. For all their vaunted Panzer spearheads, the German Army in Russia depended on horses for over 80 per cent of its motive power.

The German advance slowed amid blizzards and temperatures so low that they welded artillery pieces into immovable blocks on the rock-hard earth. Some German patrols reached a tram terminus on the outskirts of Moscow. They could see the domes of the Kremlin glinting in the sun. On 6 December the Russians counter-attacked with fresh and well-equipped divisions rushed from Siberia. They drove the German Army Group Centre back 200 miles before the offensive slithered to a halt in the glutinous mud of the spring thaw of 1942. *Blitzkrieg* had met its match.

Below: The retreat from Moscow. The German Army was ill-equipped for the rigours of the Russian winter. In the battle for Moscow the German Fourth Army's losses to frotsbite were more than twice its battle casualties.

THE BATTLE OF THE ATLANTIC

WINSTON Churchill considered that the Battle of the Atlantic was the *'dominating factor all through the war. Never could we forget that everything depended on its outcome'.* If Britain's trans-Atlantic supply line with America had been cut by the German Navy's U-boats, the British would have been unable to continue the war. The battle to defeat the submarine threat was the longest and most important fought by the British.

At first the U-boats gained the upper hand. Hunting in groups known as 'wolfpacks' and guided to their targets by long-range reconnaissance aircraft, the U-boats could stay at sea for long periods, refuelled by supply submarines. By co-ordinating surface attacks at night, they could overwhelm convoy escorts by sheer weight of numbers.

Crisis point was reached at the beginning of 1943. The U-boats were sinking ships at twice the rate they were being built, while for every U-boat sunk, two were launched. The U-boats seemed to have victory within their grasp.

Opposite: The last photograph of the British battlecruiser *Hood* as she went into action against the German pocket battleship *Bismarck*, south of Greenland, on 24 May 1941. *Hood* was sunk by plunging fire from *Bismarck*, which also damaged the battleship *Prince of Wales*, from which the photograph was taken. *Bismarck's* triumph was shortlived. She was crippled by a torpedo, dropped by a Swordfish torpedo-bomber from the carrier *Ark Royal* and on 27 May was overhauled and pounded to bits by the battleships *Rodney* and *King George V*. The 'coup de grâce' was delivered by a torpedo fired by the cruiser *Dorsetshire*. Only 107 of *Bismarck's* crew survived.

Technology turned the tide. Powerful new centimetric radars were fitted to long-range Allied aircraft equipped with searchlights and depth charges, enabling them to hunt the U-boats at night. High Frequency Direction Finding (known as 'Huff Duff') helped convoy escorts to pinpoint and shadow U-boats when they were transmitting back to base. Hunter-killer groups built around fast escort carriers took a heavy toll of U-boats.

By the summer of 1943 the tonnage of Allied shipping launched overtook that lost to the U-boats for the first time in the war. The U-boat menace had been mastered. The Germans' own technological innovations, the endurance-improving Schnorkel tube and the ocean-going Type XXI, ancestor of all modern submarines, proved too little and too late to regain the initiative.

Left: Survive the savage sea. Oil-clogged U-boat crewmen are picked up by a Royal Navy warship. The Battle of the Atlantic claimed a heavy price in lives. Some 300,000 men of the British Merchant Navy (one-fifth of its pre-war strength) fell victim to the U-boats. Casualties among U-boat crews ran at 75 per cent overall, greater by far than any other arm of service in the navy, army or air force in any combatant country.

Above: A U-boat under aerial attack. The Battle of the Atlantic was a high-technology struggle in which the advantage swung back and forth. In January-July 1942 the average life of a U-boat in the Atlantic was 13 months. By the end of the war the life expectancy of a U-boat had dwindled to three months. Of 830 U-boats despatched on operations, the German Navy lost 690, almost all of them in the Atlantic.

KEEP SMILING THROUGH: THE BRITISH HOME FRONT

NO NATION mobilized more thoroughly for war than the British. *'Don't you know there's a war on?'* were the words which rang through the conflict, from rationing queues to shell factories.

Peacetime staples quickly became luxuries. Meat rationing was introduced in March 1940, shrinking as ships went down in the Atlantic. In bad times the weekly butter ration of four ounces was halved and the cheese allowance came to resemble mousetrap bait, in size as well as quality. Nevertheless, fair shares for all meant that the diet and health of the nation improved during the war.

Below: Arrivals and departures. Troops and evacuees at a London railway station. At the beginning of the war about 1.5 million children were evacuated from Britain's cities to 'reception areas' safe from German bombs. When the bombs failed to materialize, many returned to their homes. The onset of the Blitz in September 1940 prompted a new wave of evacuation. Evacuation and the imposition of the black-out were the two main features of life on the home front during the Phoney War.

Right: The Army that never fought. A Home Guard sentry keeps watch outside London's County Hall in the summer of 1940, when a German invasion seemed imminent. Originally called the Local Defence Volunteers, the Home Guard was formed in May 1940 and by the end of June numbered some 1.5 ill-equipped but enthusiastic men. Hitler called them a 'murder band', but 'Dad's Army' had the last laugh.

The entire nation was embraced by the war effort and a substantial civilian part of it was propelled into the front line by the Blitz. In the winter of 1940 a woman Air Raid Warden in the East End was in greater physical danger every night than the majority of men serving in the forces.

The conscription of women began in December 1941. By mid-1943 nine out of ten single women were in the forces or war industry, serving as Land Girls, operating mixed anti-aircraft batteries or working as welders in Britain's shipyards. Margaret Weldon, a member of the Women's Auxiliary Air Force (WAAF) recalled: *'In a way it was like going to university. We were mostly that age and you see people change as they grow up through a war. Before the war I had never been anywhere much and I knew very little. The people I knew were confined to my local area. In the WAAF I met all kinds of people in all kinds of circumstances. I saw things I never thought I would see. And there's an instant bond between us all when we meet again today'.*

Below: A woman at work in a munitions factory. Women were quick to fill the places vacated by men serving in the forces. In the shipyards they became expert welders, particularly adept at intricate work requiring finesse and attention to detail. Even so, they were still paid less than their male colleagues.

Below: Harvest time for members of the Women's Land Army. Eventually there were some 80,000 Land Girls boosting agricultural output. About 1,000 of them worked as rat catchers. Another 6,000 joined the Timber Corps, selecting and felling trees in remote parts of the countryside and working in sawmills.

RISING SUN: JAPAN'S ROAD TO WAR

JAPAN HAD begun to intervene in mainland China in 1931, when the troops it stationed there to guard the Japanese-run railways in Manchuria took over the province. War with China followed in 1937 when the Japanese garrison guarding the embassy at Peking exchanged fire with Chinese troops before going on to the offensive.

Japan went on to occupy the entire Chinese coast and large tracts of the interior. Without military support from Britain, which allowed war materials to be transported along the 'Burma Road' to Chungking, the Chinese government, headed by Chiang Kai-shek, would have been unable to resist the Japanese.

The United States had stood aside from the Japanese expansion. But in September 1940 it was extended to French Indochina, where Vichy France granted Japan military bases from which it could threaten Malaya, the East Indies and the US protectorate of the Philippines.

President Roosevelt chose an economic weapon to halt the Japanese advance, imposing an embargo on rubber, which was followed in July 1941 by the freezing of all Japanese assets in the United States and the announcement of an oil embargo against all aggressors, including Japan. At a stroke the Japanese were deprived of 90 per cent of their oil supplies and 75 per cent of their foreign trade. The Japanese were confronted with a choice – diplomatic retreat from their Chinese conquests or war. They decided to play for time while planning a surprise attack on the US Navy.

Below: War baby. A child abandoned in the ruins of Shanghai after a Japanese air raid. The city fell to the Japanese on 8 November 1937.

Above: The battleship *Yamato*, symbol of Japanese naval might. Designed to outgun any battleship afloat, with nine 18-inch guns, the *Yamato* and her sister ship *Musashi* entered service in 1940 at a time when the aircraft carrier was becoming the capital ship of the world's naval powers. *Yamato* was sunk on 7 April 1945 by American carrier-borne aircraft while sailing on a suicide mission against the US forces invading Okinawa.

Below: Chinese civilians are executed by Japanese troops in 1937. The Japanese invasion of China and subsequent conquest of swathes of the Pacific and South-East Asia was characterized by extremes of brutality.

PEARL HARBOR: DAY OF INFAMY

AFTER THE imposition of the American oil embargo, Admiral Osami Nagano, Chief of the Japanese General Staff, observed that Japan was like *'a fish in a pond from which the water is gradually being drained away'.*

Alternative sources of raw materials were relatively near at hand, in Borneo, Java and Sumatra, Malaya and Burma. The only way to obtain them would be to undertake the rapid military conquest of a vast area of the Far East. In November 1941 talks began in Washington with the aim of averting hostilities. Meanwhile the Japanese prepared a surprise carrier strike against the US Pacific Fleet's base at Pearl Harbor on the Hawaiian island of Oahu.

Above: The destroyer *Shaw* explodes in its dry dock after a direct hit during the Japanese attack on Pearl Harbor, 7 December 1941. Shortly before 1pm on the 8th, President Roosevelt asked Congress to declare war against Japan. Britain declared war on Japan the same day. Three days later Germany and Italy – honouring treaty obligations with Japan – declared war on the United States. The British Prime Minister Winston Churchill recognized this as the turning point in the war. With the vast military potential of United States engaged against Japan *and* Germany, Churchill was convinced that the war would be won.

On 26 November the Japanese fleet left harbour. Maintaining radio silence, and under cover of clouds and squalls, it sailed to its attack positions 200 miles from Pearl Harbor. The Americans were aware of Japanese intentions; they had been decoding and reading Japanese messages for months. But they were ignorant of Japan's precise plans.

At 7.55am on 7 December the Japanese struck, achieving complete surprise. Aircraft from six carriers sank or disabled six of the battleships anchored at Pearl Harbor and destroyed over 300 aircraft on the ground. One vital factor cheated them of annihilating victory; the Pacific Fleet's two carriers were on a training cruise and escaped attack.

Below: A Japanese airman's view of 'Battleship Row' at Pearl Harbor. Of the seven battleships sunk or damaged during the raid, only two, *Arizona* and *Oklahoma*, would never sail again. *Pennsylvania*, in dry dock, escaped serious damage. Crucially, the second wave of Japanese warplanes failed to attack Pearl Harbor's dock repair and oil storage facilities, the destruction of which would have immobilized the US Pacific Fleet.

NORTH AFRICAN SEESAW 1

FOR THREE years after the fall of France, the only theatre in which the ground forces of the Western Allies were able to come to grips with the Axis was in North Africa. Commanders in the Western Desert of Egypt and Libya were as much prisoners of geography and climate as their counterparts on the Eastern Front.

The Western Desert was an arid waste yielding nothing. Over long stretches, the landward edge of the coastal plain was bounded by high ground or a steep depression which confined the movement of armies to a narrow 40-mile strip. The war in North Africa was characterized by a series of advances and retreats along this 1,200-mile-long strip, stretching from Tripoli in the west to Alexandria in the east, along which a chain of small ports were the only points of military value. The war took the form of dashes from one point of maritime supply to the next, with the aim of depriving the enemy of water, fuel, ammunition, food and reinforcements which, in that order, were the essentials of desert warfare.

The desert might seem a clean environment, but it was a cruel one for the men who fought in it. They endured broiling heat and freezing nights, flies and grit, sweat-soaked clothing and desert sores. A shower of rain could turn sand into the consistency of mud as deep and clinging as any on the Eastern Front.

Below: An Afrika Korps MkIII panzer drives through the desert during Rommel's drive to Bir Hacheim in June 1942. Its British counterpart, the Matilda infantry tank, could not compete with the MkIII and was withdrawn as a gun tank at the end of 1942. The MkIII encountered more serious opposition with the arrival in North Africa in May 1942 of the American M3 Grant tank, with its sponson-mounted 75mm gun which was capable of firing armour-piercing and high-explosive ammunition.

Left: Scourge of British armour, the German 88mm gun in action at Mersa el Brega in April 1941. An anti-aircraft gun developed by Krupp in the early 1930s, its capabilities as an anti-tank weapon were first noted during the Spanish Civil War.

Below: In a typically bleak desert landsape, littered with the detritus of war, British infantry bring in German and Italian prisoners captured in October 1942.

NORTH AFRICAN SEESAW 2

IN 1940 the British had things their own way in North Africa. Italy had declared war on Britain on 10 June 1940, and in September launched a ponderous offensive into Egypt from its North African colony in Libya. Although heavily outnumbered, the British fought a brilliant campaign to drive the Italians back 500 miles to Benghazi.

The situation underwent a rapid change in February 1941 with the arrival of the German Afrika Korps commanded by General Erwin Rommel. His brilliant handling of armour and tactic of drawing British tanks on to his formidable 88mm anti-tank guns made him a constant threat until, starved of supplies, he was bludgeoned into defeat by General Montgomery at the second Battle of El Alamein in November 1942.

Below: British infantry move forward at the second Battle of El Alamein, a bitter slogging match which was opened on 23 October 1942 by a massive bombardment from 800 British guns. The commander of the British Eighth Army, General Montgomery, enjoyed a big material advantage over his Axis opponents, and by the evening of 3 November had reduced the Afrika Korps to only 30 operational tanks. Shortly before dawn on 4 November Rommel began the long withdrawal to Tunisia.

Rommel's defeat was secured by the virtual throttling of the Axis supply lines across the Mediterranean and the quantitative superiority in material which the British Eighth Army was able to achieve by the autumn of 1942. Rommel's difficulties were exacerbated by the fact that, in Hitler's eyes, the North African theatre was always a sideshow. Nevertheless, it was not until May 1943 that the German and Italian forces in North Africa surrendered, a process hastened by the Allied landings in Morocco and Algeria in November 1942.

Below: A knocked-out German MkIII tank is captured on 29 October, a week into the second Battle of El Alamein, the decisive battle of the Desert War. The British victory was qualified by a slow pursuit of the retreating Germans, hampered by heavy rain, fuel shortages and Montgomery's characteristic caution.

Below: Desert raiders. Colonel David Stirling with one of his deep penetration raiding parties which operated far behind enemy lines in conjunction with units of the Long Range Desert Group. Stirling's creation evolved into the Special Air Service (SAS) Regiment. Stirling was captured in Tunisia in 1943 and, after many attempts to escape, finished the war in the confines of Colditz castle.

THE RED ARMY STRIKES BACK

IN THE summer of 1942 Hitler returned to business left unfinished in front of Moscow in December 1941. Once again the panzers rolled: Army Group A struck through the Donets corridor to Stalingrad while Army Group B drove through Rostov to the Caucasus and on towards the Soviet Union's southernmost oilfields at Baku on the Caspian Sea.

Below: A Red Army battalion commander leads his men into action. After its near destruction in 1941, a new battle-hardened Red Army emerged to wrest the initiative back from the Germans.

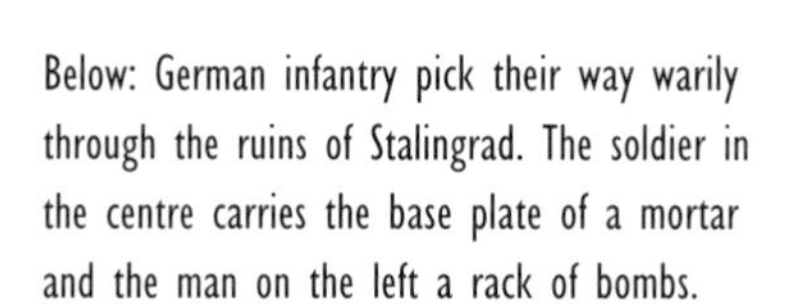

Below: German infantry pick their way warily through the ruins of Stalingrad. The soldier in the centre carries the base plate of a mortar and the man on the left a rack of bombs.

Above: The horror and the pity. The aftermath of a German atrocity in the Kerch peninsula in the Crimea captured by the great war photographer Dmitri Baltermants in 1942. Nazi ideology ensured that the war on the Eastern Front was fought with unequalled savagery. The Russians repaid their enemy in kind. By the end of 1944 there were few Red Army men who did not have a personal score to settle with the Germans.

Hitler's plan was unhinged by his growing obsession with the seizure of Stalingrad, the straggling industrial city on the banks of the Volga. Russian resistance denied him the prize and, by the winter of 1942, turned Stalingrad into a tomb for the encircled German Sixth Army. On 31 January 1943 its commander, Field Marshal Paulus, and 100,000 men went into captivity. A massive Soviet counter-attack, launched in January 1943 between Orel and Rostov, threatened Kharkov and the German forces withdrawing from the Caucasus.

The Soviet offensive was halted in its tracks by a brilliantly weighted counterblow delivered by Field Marshal von Manstein in February-March 1943. When the fighting died down in the mud of the spring thaw, it left a huge fist-shaped salient, centred around the city of Kursk, in the heartland of the Ukraine, jutting westward into the German line.

KURSK: CLASH OF ARMOUR

THE KURSK bulge exercised a horrible fascination on Hitler. He told General Guderian, Inspector of Armoured Troops, that every time he thought of the impending attack on the salient his stomach turned over.

The build-up for the operation, codenamed Citadel and aimed at clawing back the initiative after the surrender of Sixth Army at Stalingrad, took three months. The Red Army, reorganized, re-equipped and increasingly confident, had been warned of the German plans by the 'Lucy' spy network in Switzerland and agents placed in the British decoding centre at Bletchley Park (see p.80). Under the overall direction of Marshal Zhukov it prepared to defend the salient in massive strength and depth.

Below: Into the cauldron. T-34s of Fifth Guards Tank Army carry infantry into action in the Kursk salient while Illyushin Il-2 Shturmovik attack bombers flash across the sky ahead of them. Some 6,000 tanks and assault guns were drawn into the Battle of Kursk. Losses on both sides were about 1,500 armoured vehicles, but the Germans lacked the reserves to recover their strength. In contrast, Russian tank production capacity far exceeded Germany's.

When Hitler launched his tanks against the southern and northern shoulders of the Kursk salient on 5 July 1943, they were caught in the Soviet killing grounds and mangled beyond repair. No sooner had the German thrusts been contained than the Red Army delivered a series of crushing counter-attacks which by September had driven the German Army back to the line of the River Dnieper. Hitler had gambled all on the throw of a single dice and had lost the initiative on the Eastern Front, never to regain it.

Above: Red Army anti-tank riflemen under fire. No soldier was better equipped for anti-tank fighting than the Red Army infantryman. It suited his ability to hug the ground and defend his native soil to the last breath. By June 1943 the Russian infantry had received 1.5 million anti-tank rifles.

Left: The face of defeat. A German artilleryman in the Orel salient. Between July and October 1943 'irreplaceable' German losses on the Eastern Front reached 365,000, the greater part inflicted at Kursk and during the retreat to the Dnieper.

STRATEGIC BOMBING 1

IN 1940 the Luftwaffe's twin-engined bombers lacked the payload to level London and Britain's industrial cities. RAF Bomber Command was no better placed to win the war by bombing alone, the cherished hope of air strategists in the 1930s. Its aircraft groped their way blindly over a blacked-out Europe. Even on moonlit nights most of them were dropping their bombs miles from their targets.

Nevertheless, the bombing campaign remained the only way the British could strike directly at Germany. Things improved in 1942 with the arrival in numbers of four-engined bombers equipped with increasingly sophisticated radio navigation aids. This coincided with a change of policy. Although the destruction of precision targets remained an intermittent, and spectacular, feature of Bomber Command operations, most of the RAF's bombs would now fall on 'area' targets. If Bomber Command could not destroy German war factories, it could destroy the cities where the factory workers lived. Bomber Command's C-in-C, Air Chief Marshal Sir Arthur Harris, believed that the systematic destruction of Germany's cities would, by itself, bring an end to the war. All other targets, for example those linked with oil or fighter production, Harris dismissed as mere 'panaceas'.

Below: A Wellington bomber and crews of the RAF's 149 Squadron on their return from Bomber Command's raid on Berlin on 25 August 1940 which partly prompted Hitler to turn the Luftwaffe against London. Designed by Barnes Wallis, the Wellington had a geodetically constructed airframe which enabled it to sustain massive battle damage and still keep flying. The 'Wimpey' bore the brunt of Bomber Command's night offensive until the arrival of the four-engined heavy bombers, the Short Stirling, Handley Page Halifax and Avro Lancaster.

Area bombing reached a climax in July-August 1943 when, in Operation Gomorrah, Bomber Command mounted a series of devastating raids on Hamburg. A subsequent attempt to 'wreck Berlin from end to end', which lasted from November 1943 to March 1944, was abandoned after losses of nearly 500 aircraft. However, German air defences were now becoming a wasting asset, while Bomber Command's range of Pathfinding and target-marking techniques was concentrating the maximum number of aircraft over the target in the minimum amount of time. By the end of the war Germany's cities lay in ruins.

Below: A magnificent view of the Merlin engines of the Avro Lancaster, Bomber Command's best heavy bomber. With a bombload of 14,000 pounds the Lancaster had a range of 1,660 miles. Specially adapted Lancasters carried the 22,000-pound Grand Slam bomb for use against hardened targets like U-boat pens and railway viaducts.

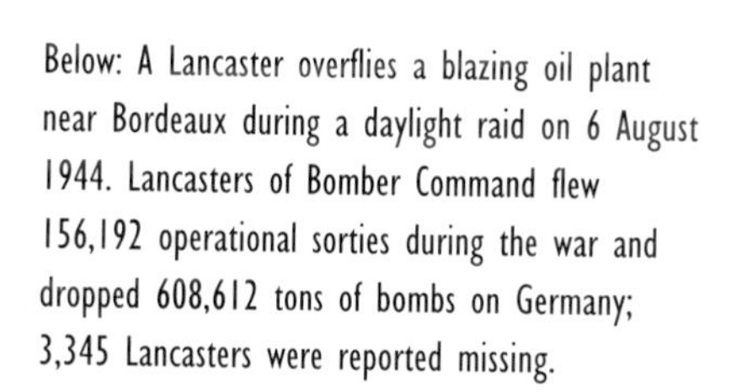

Below: A Lancaster overflies a blazing oil plant near Bordeaux during a daylight raid on 6 August 1944. Lancasters of Bomber Command flew 156,192 operational sorties during the war and dropped 608,612 tons of bombs on Germany; 3,345 Lancasters were reported missing.

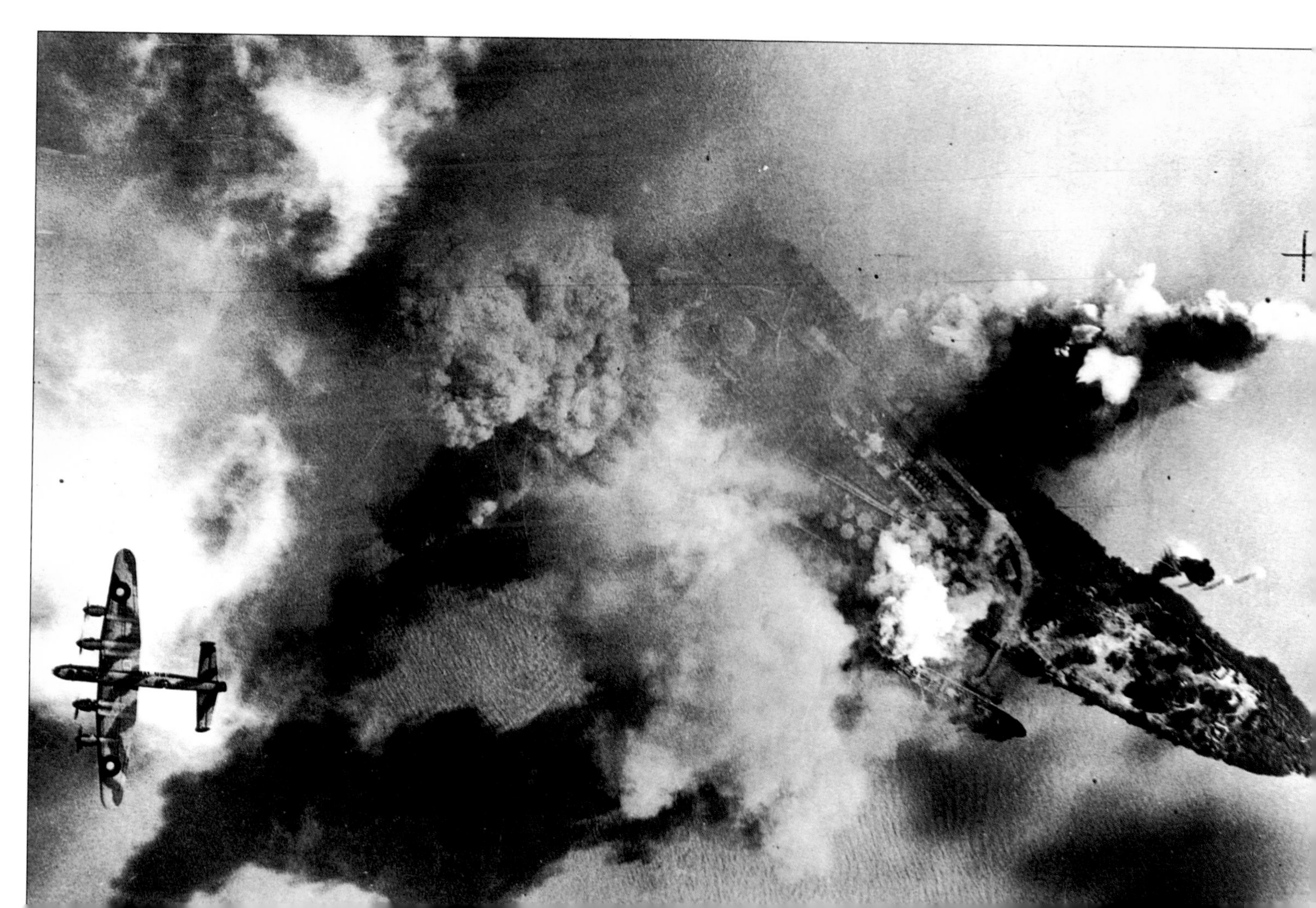

STRATEGIC BOMBING 2

WHILE THE RAF bombed Germany by night, the US Eighth Air Force, which arrived in England in the summer of 1942, bombed by day. US airmen arrived bristling with confidence that bombing would win the war.

At the core of the philosophy of the United States Army Air Force (USAAF) was the belief that high-level daylight precision bombing could destroy the key elements in the German war economy. The American bomber chiefs were convinced that, in the absence of a satisfactory long-range escort fighter, their bomber formations could fight their way to and from targets in Germany without suffering unacceptable losses. The Americans were not deterred by the fact that

Above: Boeing B-17 Flying Fortress bombers of US Eighth Air Force over Europe. Note the vapour trails of their fighter escorts. Maintaining formation required extreme concentration and physical effort from the B-17s' pilots. A 54-aircraft combat wing of 1943 was about 1.24 miles wide and half a mile deep, with 600 yards between the leading and trail aircraft in each of the wing's box-like 18-aircraft groups.

Left: A stricken B-17 of 94th Bombardment Group over Berlin, its tailplane mangled by bombs falling from aircraft flying higher in the formation. The 94th flew on the ill-fated Regensburg mission of 17 August 1943. Of 376 aircraft despatched on twin raids against war plants at Schweinfurt and Regensburg, 60 were lost and many more written off.

earlier in the war both Bomber Command and the Luftwaffe had employed these tactics and had failed.

In the skies over Germany the USAAF's theory was tested almost to the point of destruction. B-17 Flying Fortresses and B-24 Liberators, flying in mass formation, sustained increasingly heavy losses at the hands of the Luftwaffe's day fighters. By the late summer of 1943 average losses were running at 10 per cent per mission, a rate that could not be sustained, and morale had nosedived.

The crisis came to an end in December 1943 with the introduction of the formidable P-51 Mustang escort fighter, powered by a Rolls Royce Merlin engine and capable not only of escorting the bombers all the way to targets deep inside Germany but also of forming fighting patrols to sweep the skies clear of enemy fighters.

Right: Consolidated B-24 Liberators bomb Tours in France. Note the formation leader's smoke markers, which triggered simultaneous release of their bombs by the following aircraft to produce a pattern of bombs around the target. The Liberator and the Flying Fortress, both of which were heavily laden with defensive armament, could carry a 5,000-pound bombload over a range of about 2,000 miles.

Left: Suffer the little children. Refugees fleeing from the city of Dresden, in Saxony, which was destroyed in a series of raids delivered by Bomber Command and Eighth Air Force between 13 and 15 February 1945. The raids, in which up to 130,000 civilians perished, remain controversial today.

SIX MONTHS OF VICTORY

IN THE six months following Pearl Harbor, Japan cut a swathe through the Pacific, gaining vast territories for its 'Greater East Asia Co-Prosperity Sphere'. Faced with scattered, ill-equipped opposition, the Japanese secured victory with the brilliant use of intelligence, incisive central planning and the smooth co-ordination of naval, air and ground forces.

By May 1942 the territory in Japanese hands included the islands of Guam and Wake, the Philippines, French Indochina, Burma, Thailand, Malaya, Singapore, Hong Kong, the Dutch East Indies, three-quarters of New Guinea and Papua, the Bismarck Archipelago and a substantial part of the Gilbert and Solomon Islands. To the north, they threatened the Aleutian chain and the approaches to Alaska; in the west, having overrun Malaya, captured the great naval base at Singapore and bundled the

Below: Japanese landing parties storm ashore in the British colony of Hong Kong on 8 December 1941. Fighting continued until Christmas Day, when the British commander, Major-General C.M. Maltby, surrendered. The Japanese victory was followed by an orgy of killing and rape.

British out of Burma, they were close to the borders of India; to the south they menaced Australia.

The Japanese had reached the limits of conquest predicted by Admiral Yamamoto the C-in-C of the Japanese Combined Fleet. To secure their vast perimeter, they now sought to lure the US Pacific Fleet into battle and destroy it.

Above: Surrender in Singapore, 15 February 1941, the single most catastrophic defeat in British military history. Over 130,000 troops were taken prisoner.

Opposite: The doomed battleship *Prince of Wales*, which was sent to Singapore with the battlecruiser *Repulse* as the major units in Force Z. On 8 December 1941 *Prince of Wales* and *Repulse* sailed from Singapore to strike at Japanese transports supporting the landings in northern Malaya. Lacking air cover, they were sunk by Japanese level and torpedo-bombers on 10 December.

Right: Some of the 76,000 US and Filipino prisoners taken by the Japanese in the Bataan peninusla on Luzon in the Philippines. At least 20,000 of them died on the subsequent 'Death March' to their prison camp, a grim warning of the brutality meted out by the Japanese to Allied prisoners of war.

TURNING THE PACIFIC TIDE

AT THE Battle of the Coral Sea, 4-8 May 1942, the Japanese were halted and a new era in naval warfare was opened. The first large-scale aircraft carrier clash was fought without either surface fleet sighting the enemy.

At Coral Sea the Japanese sank one of Admiral Frank Fletcher's two carriers, *Lexington*, and damaged the other, *Yorktown*. Believing both carriers had been sunk, the Japanese fleet pressed on with its plan to capture the island of Midway. The Americans, who had cracked the Japanese naval code, positioned their fleet to defeat the much stronger task force which the Japanese had assembled to take Midway. In the ensuing carrier battle – one of the most decisive of the war – American dive-bombers destroyed four Japanese carriers and reversed the balance of power in the Pacific.

Below: A Douglas Dauntless dive-bomber over Wake Island. It was the Dauntless that did the most damage at Midway, either sinking or crippling four Japanese carriers. Underpowered, lacking range and exhausting to fly for any length of time, the Dauntless nevertheless managed to sink a greater tonnage of Japanese shipping than any other Allied aircraft.

Above: The US carrier *Enterprise* under attack at the Battle of Santa Cruz, 26 October 1942, an engagement during the battle for Guadalcanal which left the carrier *Hornet* a burning hulk, later sunk by the Japanese.

Above: Jungle conditions. During the operations to isolate the Japanese base at Rabaul in December 1943 a tropical downpour drenches the crew of a 75mm gun as it fires on Japanese positions on New Britain in the Bismarck Archipelago.

The Japanese were now forced to defend a vast ocean empire which might be attacked at any point by the gathering might of the American war machine. The point the Americans chose was the Solomons chain. On 7 August 1942 US Marines stormed ashore on the island of Guadalcanal. The Japanese were not cleared from Guadalcanal until February 1943, after a series of savage ground, air and sea battles which stretched American endurance to the limit.

THE PROPAGANDA WAR

IN TOWNS and cities during the war years the pedestrian was bombarded with exhortations to help the war effort in every possible way. On a short walk, one Londoner counted 48 official posters on every subject from rationing to registering for civil defence duties. In all the combatant nations these posters were the visible symbols of the war effort.

The poster was the principal instrument of persuasion and expressed, in the most direct terms, the preoccupations of a nation's leaders and the political, military and moral imperatives which drove them, from simple appeals to patriotism to the anti-Semitism of Nazi ideology. Radio, feature films and newsreels also played their part. Radio was used as a tool of 'black propaganda' by all sides, most famously by the Germans in the person of William Joyce, who broadcast Nazi propaganda from Hamburg and whose sneering mock-aristocratic tones earned him the derisive nickname of 'Lord Haw Haw'.

Right: Bomb damage in the City of London fails to disturb a banner bearing one of the most familiar slogans of wartime Britain. In the drive to achieve national self-sufficiency in food, golf courses were turned over to the plough and small back gardens came to resemble miniature farms, crammed with chicken runs and rabbit hutches. The Albert Memorial in Hyde Park was surrounded by demonstration allotments.

Above: Josef Goebbels, the demon king of the propaganda war. After the defeat at Stalingrad, Goebbels became an increasingly important figure in the drive to achieve the total mobilization of the German war economy. On 24 August 1944 he was appointed Plenipotentiary for Total War with sweeping powers. Goebbels committed suicide, with his wife and children, in Hitler's Berlin bunker on 1 May 1945.

Right: A Nazi St George vanquishes a Jewish dragon.

In Josef Goebbels, Nazi Germany possessed a master of the art of propaganda, still capable of wrong-footing his Allied opponents at the end of the war. Intoxicated with his own skills, Goebbels nevertheless failed to grasp the simple fact that even the best propaganda was no match for the military might of the Allies. In April 1945, in the ruins of Berlin, Goebbels told his subordinates: *'... in a hundred years' time they will be making a fine colour film describing the terrible days we are living through. Do you not wish to play a part in that film?'*

THE MOVIES AT WAR

THE HOLLYWOOD film factory adapted to wartime production with the minimum of disruption. The war had cut the major studios off from many of their overseas markets. But there was a huge increase in cinema audiences at home. War workers had plenty of money to spend and craved escapist entertainment.

The US government quickly grasped the importance of film as propaganda. The familiar movie genres – crime thrillers, musicals and Westerns – were adapted to accommodate popular war themes. Patriotism proved immensely profitable for the big studios like MGM, Paramount and Warner Bros.

Below: A moment from *Fires Were Started* (1943), directed by Humphrey Jennings, a lyrical tribute to the work of the Auxiliary Fire Service during the London Blitz.

Below: David Niven in *The Way Ahead* (1944) which followed a band of recruits through their training and into battle in the Western Desert. Niven, who had been a peacetime Army officer before becoming a Hollywood star, also served with distinction in north-west Europe during the closing stages of the war.

In 1943 the number of films dealing either directly or indirectly with the war, reached a peak. As the war drew to a close, there was a growing demand for pure escapism in the form of musicals or costume dramas.

Wartime revived the flagging British film industry, which produced a steady stream of stirring documentaries about the 'People's War'. These had a strong influence on mainstream features. Movies like *Millions Like Us, The Way Ahead* and *Waterloo Road* focused their attentions on the lives of ordinary soldiers and civilians and brought a new feeling of realism to British cinema. In contrast, German wartime cinema consisted of a mixture of hymns to national history and military strength, anti-Semitic tracts and frothy escapism.

Right: Gordon Jackson and Patricia Roc in *Millions Like Us* (1943), an acutely observed populist drama set in an aircraft factory which drove home the message that the British were fighting a 'People's War'.

Left: Surrounded by admiring GIs of US Ninth Army, Marlene Dietrich tucks into a sandwich 'somewhere in Germany' in February 1945. Along with many Hollywood stars, Dietrich worked tirelessly to entertain the troops serving overseas, often near the front line.

HOLOCAUST

JEWS HAD been persecuted in Germany from the moment the Nazis came to power in 1933. In 1935 the Nuremberg Laws deprived them of full German citizenship. By November 1938 about 150,000 of Germany's 500,000 Jews had emigrated, although many found refuge in countries which were within the German Army's impending reach.

The diplomatic victories of 1938-9 brought many Eastern European Jews under Nazi control. The conquest of Poland and western Russia delivered millions more into Hitler's hands. On the orders of Heinrich Himmler, chief of the SS, massacres began almost immediately. Between June and November 1941, SS *Einsatzgruppen* (task groups) killed at least one million Jews behind German lines in Russia.

Below: A round-up of Jews in the Warsaw ghetto in 1943. The ghetto, which was sealed off from the rest of the city by a high wall, contained some 430,000 people riddled with disease and afflicted by starvation. In December 1941 it was estimated that over 200,000 people in the ghetto were without food or shelter. Corpses littered the streets covered with sheets of newspaper. From the summer of 1942 the Jews in the ghetto were systematically deported to the death camp at Treblinka 80 miles west of Warsaw.

Left: A German soldier watches a blazing building during the uprising in the Warsaw ghetto, April 1943. Young Jews had armed themselves to strike back at their tormentors. About 1,000 Jewish fighters, armed with rifles, pistols and home-made bombs fought a desperate battle for a month before they were overwhelmed by tanks, flamethrowers and aircraft. It was the last act in the history of the ghetto. Only about 100 Jews survived the uprising. The rest, some 60,0000, were killed in the fighting or sent to the death camps.

Most of the Jews were killed by mass shooting, a method Himmler considered inefficient. At the Wannsee conference in January 1942 he approved the 'Final Solution to the Jewish Problem'. Jews were rounded up in the ghettos to which they had been confined and sent to death camps in the East. Here they were either killed on arrival or worked to the point of death in SS factories before being consigned to the gas chambers. This was the fate which befell some six million Jews and many non-Jews as well, most of them forced labourers who were kept alive so long as they could work.

The removal of the Jews, if not their exact fate, was a fact known to everyone in Nazi-occupied Europe. From 1942 the Allied leadership was well aware of what was happening. But the saving of the Jews was not one of the Allies' war aims. It was not until the last months of the war, when the death camps were overrun, that the people of Britain and America were confronted with the terrible truth.

Right: A triumph of German civilization. The terrible remains of Hitler's 'New Order' at the Bergen-Belsen concentration camp, liberated by British troops on 15 April 1945. Many of the dead in this mass grave had succumbed to typhus, which had raged through the camp in the closing weeks of the war. When the British arrived they found 13,000 corpses lying in the open in grotesque piles.

THE ITALIAN CAMPAIGN

AFTER CLEARING North Africa, the Allies invaded Sicily on 9 July 1943. Led by Patton and Montgomery, US Seventh and British Eighth Armies fought with great dash but could not prevent most of the island's German defenders from disengaging and slipping across the straits of Messina to mainland Italy with the greater part of their equipment.

On 25 July, Mussolini was overthrown, and on 3 September an anti-fascist Italian government signed a secret armistice with the Allies. Six days later the Allies landed on the Italian mainland at Salerno, south of Naples.

Thereafter the Allied progress up the Italian peninsula was a long, hard slog, made all the more gruelling by difficult

Above: British troops of X Corps come ashore at Salerno, south-east of Naples, in September 1943, where they met stiff resistance from two German armoured divisions. Men and machines are being disgorged from a Landing Ship Tank (LST) designed to beach and fitted with opening bow doors.

Left: A soldier of 2nd New Zealand Division brings in two German prisoners under Castle Hill at Cassino, May 1944. The monastery which dominated the battlefield at Cassino was taken by the Polish II Corps after a savage battle. The four-month struggle for this vital link in the Gustav Line cost the Allies 21,000 casualties.

terrain, missed opportunities, stiff German resistance in a series of well-fortified defensive positions, notably the Gustav Line, and the constant drain on resources in the theatre by the priority given to the Normandy invasion. In January 1944 an amphibious landing at Anzio, behind the Gustav Line, briefly opened a window of opportunity but the chance was missed.

The strongpoint in the Gustav Line at Monte Cassino was taken in May 1944, after a bitter battle, and Rome fell on 4 June. But the Allies remained outnumbered by the German forces in Italy, and it was not until 29 April 1945 that the Germans surrendered. Far from proving the 'soft underbelly' of Churchill's imagining, Italy turned into a running sore in Allied strategy.

Right: General Mark Clark, commander of US Fifth Army, rides through St Peter's Square in Rome on 4 June 1944. The ambitious Clark frequently let his liking for personal publicity cloud his operational judgement.

THE WARLORDS

THE BROAD outlines of the war were determined by four men, Hitler, Stalin, Roosevelt and Churchill. The two dictators, Hitler and Stalin, displayed some striking similarities, adopting personal regimes which turned night into day – to the exhaustion of their staffs – and immersing themselves in the minutiae of operations, frequently with disastrous results.

As the war progressed Stalin reined in these tendencies and submitted to the advice of military professionals of the highest calibre, the battle-winner Zhukov and the staff officers Vasilevsky and Antonov. Nevertheless, he remained in total control from first to last, ruling his commanders by fear, as he did the Soviet Union.

Hitler assumed personal control of operations in December 1941, but it was a role for which he was not well suited. The easy victories of 1939 and 1940 had bred in him a contempt for his generals, the majority of whom had urged caution, and a corresponding reluctance to heed their practical advice. Sooner or later, those who stood up to him were dismissed. From 1943 Hitler fought the war from the map, clinging to a strategy of holding every inch of ground and leaving his best commanders little or no room for manoeuvre.

Above: Churchill, Roosevelt and Stalin meet for the last time at Yalta in the Crimea in February 1945, when the plans for the postwar divison of Germany were finalized. By then Roosevelt was a grievously sick man. He died of a brain haemmorrhage on 12 April. Churchill, who was to be ousted in the British general election of July 1945, was gloomily coming to terms with an exhausted Britain's reduced status at the top table. In contrast, Stalin emerged from the conference triumphant, having secured the Soviet Union's dominant position in Eastern Europe and substantial concessions from Roosevelt in return for the Soviet Union's entry into the war against Japan. The Soviet Union invaded Manchuria on 8 August 1945.

Right: Hitler and Mussolini in happier times in 1938. Although Mussolini was the senior dictator, having come to power in 1922, Italy was the junior partner in her alliance with Germany. From 10 June 1940, when Mussolini declared war on Britain and France, Italy proved a grave strategic embarrassment to Hitler. Mussolini was executed by Italian partisans on 28 April 1945.

Churchill also displayed an alarming tendency to meddle in operational matters, but most of his wildcat interventions were smoothly diverted by Field Marshal Brooke, the Chief of the Imperial General Staff, whose demanding task it was to translate his boss' strategic ambitions into hard reality, given Britain's stretched resources. The bond Churchill forged with President Roosevelt was crucial in co-ordinating Anglo-US strategy. In contrast to Churchill, however, Roosevelt remained aloof from the running of the war, retaining his peacetime routine after Pearl Harbor and leaving much in the hands of his immensely able Chief of Staff, General Marshall.

Left: The Japanese Emperor Hirohito reviews his troops in 1939. An inneffectual man, more interested in marine biology than military expansion, Hirohito exercised little influence over the senior commanders who determined policy until the closing stages of the war when defeat was inevitable. After the war he was not prosecuted as a war criminal, renounced his divine status and became one of the principal instruments of the American occupation of Japan.

OCCUPATION AND RESISTANCE

CONQUEST BRINGS its own problems: among them maintaining order in conquered territories, replacing governments and reviving and exploiting economies for the conquerors' profit.

The 'New Orders' established in Asia by the Japanese and in Europe by Germany reflected these concerns. Japanese rule in its Greater East Asia Co-Prosperity Sphere was harsh and often arbitrary but it was overshadowed by the cruelty of Germany's policy towards its conquered territories, driven as it was by Nazi racial policy. The victims were not only Jews or the millions of Russians forcibly transported to the Reich as slave labour. In Poland the German aim was not merely to dominate

Below: A German sentry stands guard on the Atlantic Wall, symbol of Hitler's 'Fortress Europe'.

but also to destroy the Polish national identity. The entire population were to become German slaves, forming a huge pool of cheap labour. In Greece, thousands starved when the Germans commandeered the food stocks.

In Occupied Europe, geography was one of the principal determinants of effective resistance. In the mountains of Yugoslavia, Marshal Tito's partisan army tied down large numbers of German and Italian divisions. In the Pripet marshes of Russia, thousands of guerrillas harassed the Wehrmacht. In small, flat Denmark, where the spirit of Resistance was strong, such operations were impossible. Churchill hoped that in the West the Resistance, with British help, would *'set Europe ablaze'.* Ultimately, its effect was psychological rather than military, although during the Normandy invasion the French Resistance played a significant disruptive role behind German lines.

Below: Members of the French Resistance in action during the liberation of Paris, August 1944.

Opposite: A firing squad executes partisans in the Balkans. In December 1941 Hitler issued his 'Night and Fog' decree, whereby inhabitants of Occupied Europe who were deemed to 'endanger German security' but were not to be immediately executed, were to disappear into limbo. No news of their fate was to be released to their families. No one knows how many people were victims of this order.

Right: Legacy of occupation. Police lead a suspected collaborator away from a vengeful crowd in liberated Paris. In the immediate aftermath of liberation thousands of collaborators were summarily executed by the Resistance. Later thousands more were tried and sentenced to death or varying terms of imprisonment.

THE GERMAN HOME FRONT

HITLER'S WAR plans had envisaged a series of short, sharp campaigns. No preparations had been made to fight the 'Total War' which the British had embraced from 1940. Sweeping German victories in France and Russia spared most Germans many of the hardships of war. Goods of all kinds flooded in from the conquered territories. Until 1941 the peacetime routines of work, school and annual holidays were not disturbed.

German war industry marked time while the wives of soldiers away at the war lived comfortably off their state allowances. It was not until 1941 that any attempt was made to direct women into war factories. However, rationing and shortages began to bite in 1942 as Allied bombers brought German civilians into the front line and losses mounted on the Eastern Front.

Below: A German soldier lends a hand on the farm in 1943. Germans had experienced their first wartime food crisis in the winter of 1941-2, caused by lack of farm workers (called up for the attack on the Soviet Union) and freight cars (now used to supply the Eastern Front).

It was not until the beginning of 1943, when the tide was already turning against Germany, that Germany mobilized to fight 'Total War' under the overall direction of Josef Goebbels, Hitler's propaganda chief. Even then the war economy remained a mass of contradictions, with six million workers still producing consumer goods and 1.5 million women employed as maids and cooks. Corruption and waste, bred by the warring Nazi Party fiefdoms encouraged by Hitler as a means of preserving his own authority, bedevilled the German home front to the end of the war. The whole system would have collapsed had it not been for the millions of slave workers transported to Germany from Eastern Europe.

Above: Ration cards are distributed to bombed-out civilians. The actress Hildegard Kneff, who grew up in wartime Berlin, remembered the diet of the mid-war years – weak ersatz coffee, margarine on rolls and 'powdered eggs, diluted and stirred, scrambled and fried and tasting of glue'.

Above: A mobile kitchen provides a warming jug of soup for an air raid victim. From 1943 Allied bombers inflicted increasingly heavy damage on Germany's cities. Two-thirds of Hamburg's population were evacuated after the fire raids of August 1943; as the end of the war approached every third house in Berlin had been destroyed or rendered uninhabitable.

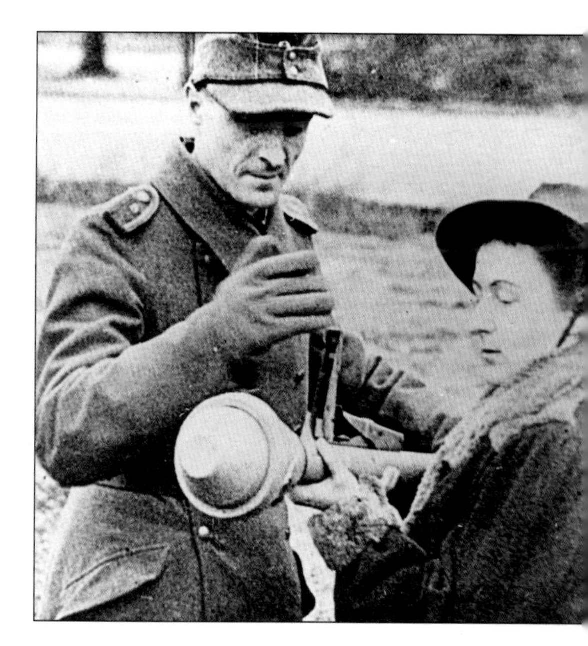

Right: Desperate measures. As the Russians close on Berlin a housewife receives instructions in the use of the Panzerfaust, a hand-held recoilless anti-tank weapon.

THE YANK INVASION

THE FIRST American troopship docked in Belfast on 26 January 1942, only seven weeks after the Japanese attack on Pearl Harbor. During the next three years nearly 1.5 million GIs – their equipment stamped 'GI' for General Issue – passed through Britain en route to Europe or to serve on bomber and fighter bases.

The Americans burst upon drab wartime Britain with all the brash vigour of a Technicolor Hollywood movie. One young woman recalled the arrival of American troops near Bournemouth: *'They swaggered, they boasted and they threw their money about, bringing a shot in the arm to business . . . and an enormous lift to the local female population.'*

They were not so popular with the local men, and British troops, who reflected that the Americans were *'overpaid, oversexed and over here'*. A US Army private drew ten shillings a day compared with the Tommy's two. GIs could afford to give girls a better time and

Below: GIs aquaint themselves with the British tea ceremony. Each GI had a little booklet, *A Short Guide to Britain*, the advice in which included: 'If you are invited to eat with a family, don't eat too much. Otherwise you might eat up their weekly rations. . . Don't try to tell the British that America won the last war or make wisecracks about the war debts or British defeats in this war'. For their part, the British welcomed the Americans, but were a little puzzled by the strict colour bar which operated in their armed forces.

shower them with cigarettes and nylons from their well-stocked PX stores. Small wonder that 'GI fever' swept Britain, from the American club at 'Rainbow Corner' in London's Piccadilly Circus to the smallest country hamlet. By D-Day 20,000 British women had become 'GI brides'. A less agreeable associated phenomenon was a soaring VD rate. By then, however, the Americans were moving on, into Europe, leaving many longing hearts behind.

Above: Men of an American armoured division are briefed before the D-Day landings. By June 1944 south-eastern and western England were so packed with men and material that the troops joked that if the invasion did not come soon, the island would sink.

Right: Hi, honey, you're home! US Marine Francis M. Connolly greets his British war bride Toni and their son Kenneth as they arrive with other GI brides in New York in February 1946.

THE RED ARMY ROLLS ON

BETWEEN DECEMBER 1943 and June 1944, a series of Soviet offensives drove the Germans out of the Crimea and the Ukraine and back into eastern Poland. While the struggle in Normandy in the days after D-Day absorbed Hitler and the Western Allies, the Red Army was gathering itself for a renewed attack.

Operation Bagration, named after Napoleon's Russian adversary in 1812, opened on 22 June, the third anniversary of Barbarossa. The offensive tore great holes in the front held by the German Army Group Centre. When the offensive finally ran down in August as it approached the River Vistula, it had punched a 250-mile gap in the German line, advanced 450 miles to the Gulf of Riga and the borders of East Prussia and destroyed the equivalent of 25 enemy divisions. The German Army Group Centre had been smashed and Army Group North isolated on the Baltic coast, where it was to remain, cut off, for the rest of the war. The German Army on the Eastern Front had been dealt a blow from which it would never recover.

Below: A massive column of German prisoners trudge wearily through the streets of Moscow. From Kursk (July 1943) to the final assault on Berlin the story on the Eastern Front was one of Russian advance and German retreat. The Red Army was to remain in undisputed possession of the initiative.

Bagration had brought the Red Army to the gates of Warsaw, where on 1 August 1944 the Polish Home Army rose up against the Germans. The Red Army did not come to the aid of the Poles but stood by while the Germans suppressed the uprising with great brutality. The Germans were not driven out of the Polish capital until January 1945.

Left: Soviet artillery, hammer of the German Army in the East. Drawing on a huge strategic reserve, the Red Army's artillery chief, Marshal Voronov, was able to mass crushing concentrations of guns in key sectors.

Below: T-34/85s in action with Marshal Malinovsky's Third Ukrainian Front west of Odessa in April 1944. In the Russian offensive of the first four months of 1944 the Red Army recovered the Ukraine and drove the Germans back to the Carpathians and almost to the borders of Poland.

Below: A salvo from a battery of Katyusha ('Little Kate') rocket launchers. A Red Army Katyusha division was capable of firing a barrage of 3,840 fin-stabilized rockets (230 tons of high explosive) up to a range of 3.5 miles. The Germans dubbed the Katyushas 'Stalin organs'.

OVERLORD

ANXIOUS TO deploy their massive resources, the Americans had urged the invasion of north-west Europe as early as the spring of 1943. The British, fearful of heavy losses, sought to postpone a landing until Allied air power had weakened the Germans.

In the summer of 1942 the British headed off an American plan for a 48-division invasion of northern Europe planned for April 1943. Thereafter, Britain and the US focused their immediate attention on clearing North Africa, and the invasion of Italy, which the British believed would draw troops away from France and pave the way for their planned cross-Channel invasion.

The Russians, suffering terrible casualties, wanted an immediate invasion – Stalin's 'second front'. In early 1943 Churchill and Roosevelt agreed to accelerate the build-up of US troops in Britain. However, to Stalin's displeasure, the operation was not to be launched before the middle of 1944.

The invasion of Normandy, codenamed *Overlord*, began on 6 June 1944. After a month-long air offensive and an Allied deception plan which convinced Hitler that the main attack would come in the Pas de Calais, where he held back a powerful armoured reserve, the largest amphibious operation in history got underway.

In the small hours of 6 June, Allied airborne troops landed to seize bridges and coastal batteries on the flanks of the invasion zone. The first Allied troops came ashore at 6.30pm. On only one of the five invasion beaches did the Germans mount fierce resistance. On Omaha Beach the US V Corps took heavy casualties from experienced and well-dug-in infantry. When they broke out of their beachhead on 'Bloody Omaha', V Corps left 2,400 dead behind them.

By midnight on 6 June 57,500 US and 75,000 British and Canadian troops had been landed. It took six weeks of hard fighting before the Allies were able to break out into Normandy and trap 50,000 retreating Germans in the Falaise pocket. Paris was liberated on 25 August 1944.

Opposite: Gliders litter the Normandy landscape after the airborne landings which preceded the assaults on the five target beaches. The parachute and glider-borne troops were scattered over wide stretches of country, many of them miles from their drop zones, but succeeded in sowing confusion among the German defenders of Normandy.

Above: Men of US V Corps come ashore at Omaha Beach, Normandy, on 6 June 1944. The fight for Omaha claimed 2,400 American lives. Private 'Buster' Hamlett of the 116th Infantry Division, who was wounded during the fighting, recalled the aftermath; 'As I painfully walked back to the beach, thousands of bodies were lying there. You could walk on the bodies, as far as you could see along the beach, without touching the ground'.

Right: An American infantryman and tank in the Normandy countryside, whose chequerboard of small fields, thick hedges and sunken lanes provided the perfect terrain for ambush.

Left: Men of the South Lancashire Regiment move up Sword Beach and on to capture strongpoints at Hermanville-sur-Mer, about half a mile inland. In the background the wounded receive first aid at the water's edge.

HITLER'S REVENGE WEAPONS

IN THE small hours of 13 June 1944 a small, pilotless aircraft with stubby wings chugged across the English Channel and plunged to earth about 25 miles from London. There was a huge explosion but no casualties. The first of Adolf Hitler's Vergeltungswaffen, or Revenge Weapons, had arrived in England.

Developed by the Luftwaffe, the V-1 (classified FZG-76 by the Germans) was cheap and easy to produce and was guided to its target by a gyroscopic automatic pilot. The Germans planned to bombard London with 500 V-1s each day. The flying-bomb was not particularly accurate, but London was a very big target. By the end of August 1944 approximately 21,000 people in the London region had been killed or seriously injured by the 'doodlebugs', as the V-1s were dubbed. A new wave of evacuation began. At night thousands sheltered in the Tube, as they had done during the Blitz.

By the autumn of 1944 the V-1-menace had been overcome by fast fighter aircraft, massed anti-aircraft batteries firing shells armed with proximity fuses and the capture by the Allies of the V-1 launching sites in northern France. Then, on 8 September, a new menace appeared – the V-2 rocket, developed by the German Army and designated the A-4.

The V-2 could not be shot down, nor did it give any warning of its approach, climbing to about 75 miles before hurtling to earth at four times the speed of sound. In all, 1,115 V-2s fell on England, 517 of them in the London area. Over 1,000 V-2s were also fired by the Germans at the port of Antwerp during the closing months of the war, to deny the Allies the use of its harbour.

On 27 March 1945 the last V-2 to reach England exploded in Kent. Two days later the last V-1 fell to earth about 20 miles from London. The V-weapons had caused extensive damage and killed nearly 9,000 people in Britain. They had given the British a nasty few months and had forced the Allies to devote considerable resources to deal with them. But none of this had halted the build-up of forces in Europe or broken civilian morale.

Below: A V-1 plunges to earth in central London. What made the V-1 particularly terrifying was the fact that it could be clearly heard approaching. When the doodlebug's guidance system told its motor to stop, there was 15 seconds' silence before it dropped out of the sky. If the engine cut out after the V-1 had flown overhead, you were safe. If not, the 15-second silence might be your last.

Left: Rescue teams at the site of a V-2 incident at London's Farringdon Market, 8 March 1945. Five days later a V-2 fell on Smithfield Market on a busy morning, killing 233 people.

Above: The V-2 rocket on its mobile launcher, which enabled it to be fired from almost any level piece of ground. The V-2 could carry a ton of explosives over a range of 200 miles. But each V-2 was at least 20 times more expensive for the Germans to produce than the V-1.

RACE TO THE RHINE

ON 15 August 1944 the Allies landed in the South of France, capturing Toulon and Marseilles two weeks later. In the north they raced into the Low Countries, liberating Brussels on 3 September. On 11 September American patrols crossed the German border near Aachen.

Hopes that the war would be over by Christmas were soon dashed. A bold airborne attempt to turn the northern end of the West Wall, the German defensive line running along the Dutch and French borders, came to grief at Arnhem. The British failed to clear the Scheldt estuary, which denied Allied shipping the use of the vital port of Antwerp until November 1944. In the great forests on the German frontier, the Reichswald and the Hürtgen, there was fighting reminiscent of the slogging matches of the First World War.

Above: A MkVI Tiger tank destroyed near Caen during the breakout from the Normandy bridgehead. The Tiger, introduced in 1942, was ponderous in a fast-moving battle but heavily protected and armed with the potent 88mm gun. It often took at least half a dozen US M4 Sherman medium tanks, the mainstay of British and American armoured divisions, to knock out a cornered Tiger.

Left: American anti-aircraft guns flank the approaches to the railway bridge over the Rhine at Remagen, which was seized by advanced units of US First Army's 9th Armoured Division on 7 March 1945 after German engineers had failed to blow it. The bridge collapsed into the river ten days later.

In December 1944 Hitler launched his last great offensive in the West. It fell in the Ardennes, the scene of his triumph in 1940, but this time he lacked the resources to engineer a second Dunkirk. In March 1945 the Allies closed up to the Rhine, and in a series of crossings broke into the heartland of the Reich, isolating the German Army Group B in the ruins of the industrial region of the Ruhr.

Right: Men of British 6th Airborne Division moving away from their Horsa gliders after landing east of the Rhine on 24 March 1945. The airborne landings were part of Operation Plunder, Field Marshal Montgomery's meticulously planned crossing of the Rhine at Wesel.

Below: The men of a defeated army. German prisoners taken by the British 21st Army Group in March 1945. In the West tens of thousands of German troops were surrendering *en masse*. In the East, they were preparing a last-ditch struggle against the Red Army, now readying itself for the final drive on Berlin, the 'Lair of the Fascist Beast'.

THE FORGOTTEN ARMY: THE BURMA CAMPAIGN

THE LOSS of Burma deprived the British of the use of the 'Burma Road', along which supplies had been passed to the Chinese generalissimo Chiang Kai-shek. His fight against the Japanese, however ineptly conducted, was the principal means of drawing enemy forces away from the war in the Pacific.

The first British attempt to regain access to the Burma Road was launched in the Arakan, the steamy coastal region of northern Burma on the Bay of Bengal, at the end of 1942. It was repulsed with almost contemptuous ease by the Japanese in March-May 1943. Nevertheless, morale was boosted by the success of an irregular operation mounted behind enemy lines by the Chindits, a deep-penetration force led by the brilliant, eccentric General Orde Wingate.

In December 1943 a second offensive was launched in the Arakan by British Fourteenth Army under the leadership of the highly capable General William Slim. It was supported by a second Chindit operation and an offensive in China directed by the American General Stilwell. However, in mid-March 1944 the Japanese Fifteenth Army went on the attack, threatening India with an invasion through the frontier posts of Imphal and Kohima.

Above: Japanese infantry present arms to the rising sun on the Indo-Burmese border. Allied troops had to learn to master the Japanese in their own element, the jungle, where the war was as much a battle against the jungle itself as the enemy. Casualties from malaria during the early part of the campaigns in Burma were far higher than those sustained in battle. Later the Allies profited from the use of antibiotics which were not available to their Japanese enemy.

In two epic battles for Imphal and Kohima the Japanese were decisively defeated and driven back to the River Chindwin, which Slim crossed in December 1944. He completed the destruction of Fifteenth Army at Meiktila in March 1945 and recaptured Rangoon, the Burmese capital, on 3 May. Burma had been reconquered and the Japanese withdrew in disorder towards Thailand.

Left: Jungle fighters. These 'Chindits' were members of long-range penetration groups formed by the then Brigadier Orde Wingate for air-supplied operations behind Japanese lines in Burma. Their name derives from their arm badge of a *chinthe* or stone lion which guards the entrance to Burmese temples. In the field the Chindits were divided into 300-strong self-supporting 'columns', each with its own mule train, heavy weapons and a signals detachment drawn from the RAF. The wounded Chindit in this photograph is lucky. Many wounded had to be left behind.

Below: Air power was vital to Allied victory in the Far East. Air drops sustained the Chindits and the defenders of Imphal and Kohima. Powerful fighters like these American Republic P47 Thunderbolts flown by the RAF were fitted with long-range tanks to enable them to strike deep into Burma to seek out air and ground targets. The Thunderbolt was a rugged aircraft with excellent speed and rate of roll. It could take a tremendous amount of damage and still bring its pilot home.

ARSENAL OF DEMOCRACY

THE WAR could not have been won without the massive material contribution made by American industry. The American genius for mass production was one of the Allies' most important weapons.

From March 1941 the United States supplied the British with weapons and war materials under the terms of the Lend-Lease Act. After the United States entered the war, the aid was extended to the Soviet Union. Over the next three years the United States provided its allies with civil and military aid sufficient for them to equip 2,000 infantry divisions. The key to victory in Europe and the Pacific lay in the sheer size and efficiency of the American economy, which applied the latest business methods to war production and the rapid expansion of the US armed forces.

In 1939 the United States manufactured only a small amount of military equipment for its own needs. By 1944 it was producing no less than 40 per cent of the world's armaments. In 1940 only 346 tanks had been built in the USA; in 1944 alone 17,500 rolled off the production lines. Figures for aircraft production leapt from 2,141 in 1940 to 96,318 in 1944.

Below: Liberty Ships nearing completion on the Pacific coast. Built as a mass-production riposte to the heavy loss of shipping in the Battle of the Atlantic, they were of simple, standardized construction, displacing 10,500 tons deadweight and driven by a single screw at a speed of 11 knots. By 1945 nearly 3,000 Liberty Ships had been built, seeing service in the Atlantic and Mediterranean and with the US Navy's massive fleet trains in the Pacific. Ironically, the basic design for these immensely useful craft had been produced by a shipping company in Sunderland, England, in 1879.

One wartime Ford plant employed 42,000 people. Much of their output was bound for the Soviet Union, which by 1945 had taken delivery of nearly 500,000 US-made trucks and jeeps. Red Army soldiers advanced on Berlin in American trucks or marched westwards in American boots, 15 million pairs of which went to the Soviet Union. Soviet war production was boosted by US machine tools, high-grade petroleum, steel, copper and rail locomotives and track. Shipping losses in the Battle of the Atlantic were offset by the construction of 3,000 Liberty Ships, general-purpose freighters whose average construction time was only 42 days. One Liberty Ship was built in just five days. The war years laid the foundation of American economic and industrial pre-eminence in the postwar era.

Left: A patriotic appeal to buy war bonds to safeguard the next generation. During the war the US economy surged ahead, with the gross national product rising by 60 per cent, providing most Americans with unparalleled prosperity.

Below: Women at work on the fuselage of the B-29 Superfortress bomber in the Boeing plant at Seattle on the Pacific coast. Women found new opportunities in the aircraft plants, where they often made up over 50 per cent of the workforce. The net effect was to bring a permanent increase in the proportion of women in the labour force.

THE INTELLIGENCE WAR

ONE OF the greatest Allied technical triumphs of the war was won, not on the battlefield, but in the English countryside at Bletchley Park, the home of the British Government Code and Cypher School.

It was here that the British deciphered the top-secret German signals encoded on their Enigma machines, one of which had found its way into British hands in 1939. British radio interception networks listened to the apparently meaningless groups of letters encoded by Enigma and transmitted in Morse code. They were taken down and sent to Bletchley, where the secret of Enigma was unlocked by matching electro-mechanical computers to the electric wiring of the Enigma machine. In this way British decoders discovered the Enigma keys, the settings that were changed three times a day. Eventually many Enigma signals were being read at the same speed by the British as the Germans.

Right: General Heinz Guderian, commander of XIX Panzer Corps, in his armoured command vehicle in France in 1940. In the foreground is a German Enigma code machine with its typewriter keyboard. Inside the machine was a complex system of gears, electric wiring and a series of drums. Each of the drums carried an alphabet on the outside. Any letter typed on the Enigma keyboard could be transposed into an infinite variety of different letters by the drums inside. The Germans were convinced that Enigma's coded messages, from which no apparent pattern could be discerned, were unbreakable.

Information from the deciphered Enigma signals was codenamed Ultra. It ranged from routine orders to detailed battle plans. Ultra was surrounded by the greatest secrecy to prevent the Germans discovering that the code had been broken. The British shared Ultra with the Americans but only provided their Soviet allies with summaries of Ultra-derived information. But there was at least one Soviet spy at Bletchley. This was John Cairncross, who provided Soviet intelligence with a detailed picture of Ultra. To the end of the war, the Germans never realized that the supposedly unbreakable Enigma code had been cracked.

Below: The Japanese carrier *Hiryu* ablaze at the Battle of Midway, June 1942. Long before Japan had entered the war, US Navy codebreakers had broken its naval and diplomatic codes. Information from these codes, distributed under the codename Magic, played a key role in American victory at Midway.

Below: Admiral Yamamoto (right), commander of the Japanese Combined Fleet. In April 1943 intercepted and decoded Japanese signals enabled American fighters to intercept and shoot down Yamamoto while he was on a tour of inspection in the western Pacific.

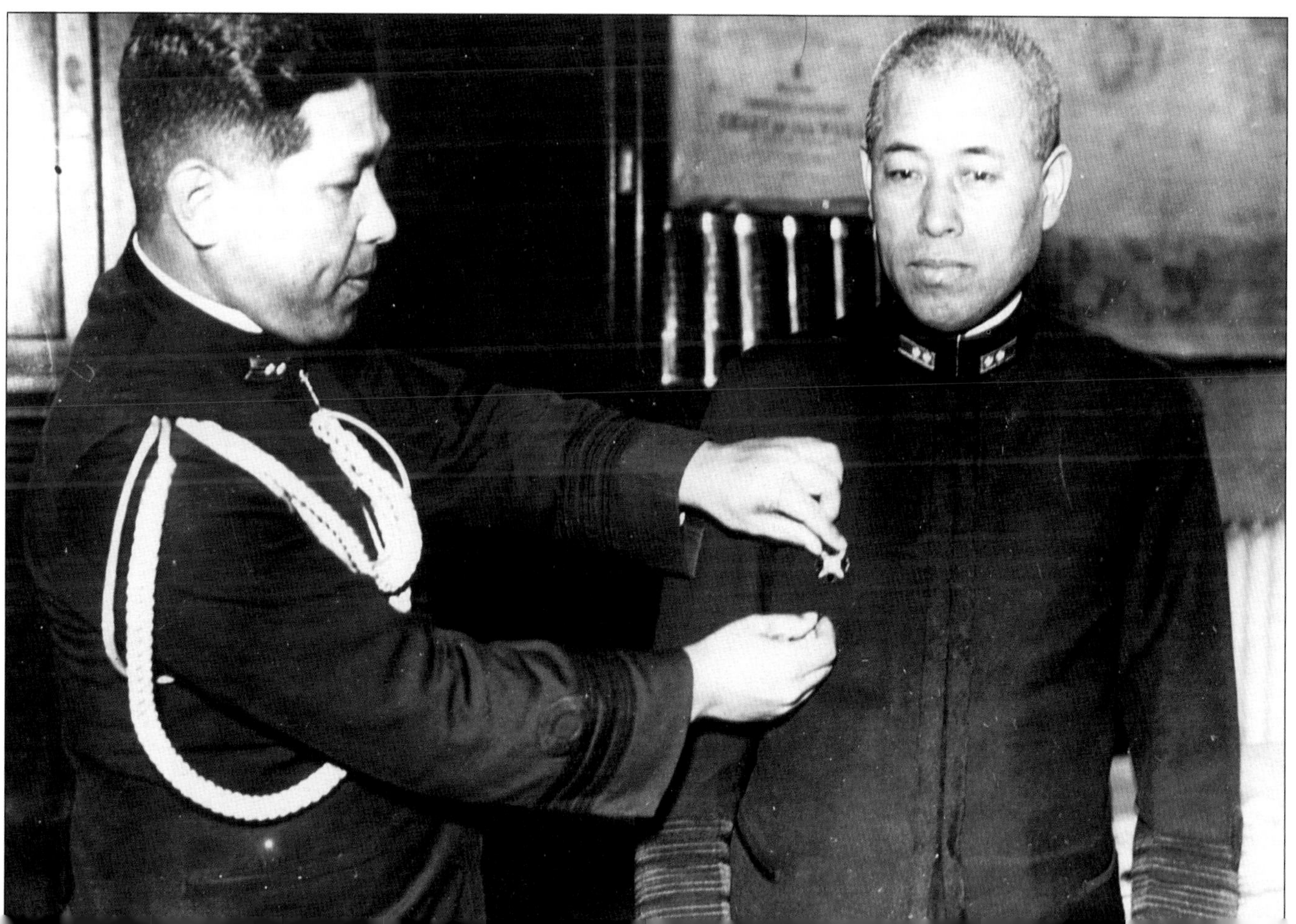

THE COMMANDERS

THE WAR threw up many military leaders with markedly different command styles. Their strengths and weaknesses continue to be debated and dissected by military historians and will provide a source of controversy for years to come.

For the Western Allies it was essential that the top positions were occupied by men who were diplomats as well as soldiers. These qualities were combined in the person of the American General Dwight D. Eisenhower, the Supreme Commander Allied Forces Europe from December 1943. 'Ike' was no fighting general but his emollient qualities held together a coalition in which temperamental subordinates like Patton and Montgomery sometimes seemed to be more at war with each other than the enemy.

Below: General Dwight D. Eisenhower with men of the US 101st Airborne Division a few hours before the launching of the invasion of Normandy. Eisenhower remains the epitome the managerial commander.

Both Patton and Montgomery were anything but diplomatic, but they inspired enormous confidence in their troops, as did Monty's brilliant opponent Rommel, the 'Desert Fox', one of the few genuinely romantic figures of the war and a general who liked to lead from the front, as did the armoured expert Guderian. On the German side, however, the outstanding operational commander was, without doubt, von Manstein, the man responsible for Hitler's decision to strike through the Ardennes in 1940 and the Red Army's most formidable enemy on the Eastern Front, where he was the master of the crushing counterstroke against a Russian breakthrough.

Three commanders stand out from the rest: the Japanese Yamamoto, the American MacArthur and the Russian Zhukov. Admiral Yamamoto was the mastermind behind the attack on Pearl Harbor who had the foresight to guarantee the Emperor Hirohito only six months of victory. General Douglas MacArthur's wartime career began with the loss of the Philippines, from which he recovered to display a masterly grasp of the possibilities of combined operations in the Pacific. Vain, tactless and domineering, MacArthur was nonetheless a commander of tactical skill and strategic vision. The third of the great commanders was Marshal of the Soviet Union Georgi Zhukov, who for much of the war, as Deputy Supreme Commander-in-Chief, was second only to Stalin in military affairs. Zhukov was Stalin's battle-winner: at Moscow in December 1941; at Stalingrad a year later; at Kursk in the summer of 1943 and thence all the way to the battle for Berlin in April 1945.

Left: Master of amphibious warfare. General Douglas MacArthur with his trademark corncob pipe and, as usual, plenty of cameramen in attendance.

Opposite: General (later Field Marshal) Montgomery at El Alamein in his Grant command tank. Montgomery's flair for publicity was coupled with an immensely painstaking approach to the waging of war and insistence on the accumulation of maximum strength before the opening of an attack. Frequently criticized for over-caution, he was nevertheless the British Army's supreme battle-winner.

Above: Field Marshal Erwin Rommel, a charismatic figure who met a tragic end. Suspected of complicity in the attempt to assassinate Hitler at his East Prussian headquarters on 20 July 1944, Rommel was offered the choice between taking poison and a show trial. Rommel chose the poison and was buried with full military honours.

Below: Marshal Zhukov on the steps of the Reichstag after the fall of Berlin. Although by Soviet standards Zhukov was economical with the lives of the millions of men under his command, he nevertheless brought a ruthlessness to the battlefield which would have been unacceptable to the Western Allies.

ASSAULT ON BERLIN

On 12 January 1945 the Red Army burst out of its bridgeheads on the Vistula and drove to the line of the Oder, bringing Zhukov's First Belorussian Front to within 50 miles of Berlin. Fleeing before the Red Army onslaught was a tidal wave of ethnic German refugees, driven from their homes in the East.

Hitler had declared Berlin a fortress, but it was a stronghold which existed only in his imagination, defended by shattered formations and the boys and old men of the German Home Guard, the Volkssturm.

On 16 April, after massive preparations, Stalin launched his final drive on Berlin, secure in the knowledge that the British and Americans had abandoned the race to seize the German capital. By 27 April Berlin's defenders had been squeezed into a narrow east-west corridor about three miles wide and twelve miles long.

The city was cut off from the outside world. Russian shells plunged down on the city centre, shaking the underground bunker in which Hitler had taken refuge. On 30 April the Führer committed suicide in the bunker. On the afternoon of 2 May General Weidling, the commander of what was left of Berlin's garrison, surrendered to the Red Army. A general surrender of German forces followed on 7 May, at Eisenhower's HQ at Rheims, and on 8 May to Zhukov in Berlin.

Left: Russian armour rolls into Berlin. In taking the city the Red Army lost nearly 305,000 men killed wounded and missing, the heaviest casualties it suffered in any battle during the war. At least 100,000 German soldiers and civilians died in the battle.

Above: The Red flag flies over the Reichstag, which fell to the Russians on 30 April 1945. Only 200 yards away Hitler and his mistress Eva Braun had committed suicide in the Führerbunker. On 25 April US and Russian troops had met at Torgan on the Elbe.

Left: Last-ditch defenders of the Reich. Men of the Berlin Volkssturm, many of them armed with Panzerfausts, are mustered in December 1944. All males between the ages of 16 and 60 who were not in the armed forces but were capable of bearing arms were liable for service in the Volkssturm.

Right: The boy defenders of the Third Reich. Members of the Hitler Youth captured by the Russians during the Battle of Berlin.

VE-DAY

BY THE spring of 1945 the end of the war seemed to have been a very long time coming. With the announcement of Hitler's death, expectations of victory in the West were raised to fever pitch, but still people were kept waiting.

The reason was an agreement between the the Allies not to announce that peace had broken out until the Germans had signed instruments of surrender in Rheims and Berlin. A tight control was kept on the journalists in Rheims, but this did not prevent an enterprising Associated Press man breaking the story. News of the German surrender reached New York on 7 May. Eisenhower, the Supreme Allied Commander, was mad but the population of the Big Apple went berserk. That night, on British radio, it was announced that 8 May would be Victory in Europe Day and a public holiday.

Below: Queen Elizabeth, King George VI and Winston Churchill, flanked by Princess Elizabeth and Princess Margaret, make one of their many VE-Day appearances on the balcony at Buckingham Palace.

In Britain, street parties and bonfires, both long in preparation, were the principal features of the VE-Day celebrations. Hitler went up in smoke on many a suburban funeral pyre, the flames kindling memories of the Blitz. The lights that blazed in towns and cities that night alarmed many small children who had grown up with the blackout.

The joy was tinged with the sadness caused by the loss of loved ones in six years of conflict, and the awareness that there was a still a war to be won in the Far East.

Left: Crowds swarm over a truck in central London during the VE-Day celebrations. The British were jubilant but would soon be feeling the effects of 'the morning after'. Britain had virtually bankrupted herself fighting the war and in the words of the economist John Maynard Keynes was facing a 'financial Dunkirk'.

Right: While Europe rejoices at the end of of an evil tyranny, two elderly Berliners contemplate the ruins of the Third Reich.

ACROSS THE PACIFIC

AFTER THE clearing of Guadalcanal the Allied Pacific drive leapfrogged towards Japan in a strategy dubbed 'island hopping'. One by one the island stepping stones across the ocean were seized by Allied forces while the major Japanese bases were isolated and left to 'wither on the vine'. The final attacks on the Japanese home islands were to be launched from the Philippines through Okinawa, from the Marianas through Iwo Jima, and from the Aleutians.

The US Marine Corps, which was in the forefront of these amphibious operations, encountered fanatical resistance. On the atoll of Tarawa, taken after bitter fighting in

November 1943, only 146 Japanese surrendered out of a garrison of nearly 5,000 men. In February-March 1945 the capture of Iwo Jima, an island a mere eight miles square, claimed nearly 7,000 American lives and left 19,000 wounded. A similar number of US troops died in the fight for Okinawa, the scene of one of the grimmest battles of the Pacific war, in which 110,00 Japanese soldiers and 150,000 civilians died, many of them preferring suicide to capture.

Above: US Marines race across open ground at Tarawa, November 1943. Tarawa was surrounded by a high reef on which many landing craft ran aground, leaving men a long wade ashore under murderous fire. Learning from the losses at Tarawa, the Marine Corps stepped up the production of amphibious tracked vehicles (amtracs), capable of powering ashore and across heavily defended beaches before disembarking the troops they carried.

The Pacific drive provoked a series of furious naval battles in which the Japanese Navy was broken on the anvil of American air power. By mid-1944 all 15 of the Japanese carriers brought into service since 1941 had been sunk or put out of action by the US Navy.

Right: US Marines hug the black sand of Iwo Jima, scene of one of the grimmest battles in the Pacific war. Iwo Jima was less than two hours' flying time to Japan, making it a key objective in the drive towards the Japanese home islands. The island, dominated by Mount Suribachi, which rises behind the men in on the beach, was heavily fortified and defended to the death by a garrison of 22,000 Japanese troops of whom only 212 chose to surrender.

Below: Amtracs churn towards Okinawa, 1 April 1945, while the 16-inch guns of a US battleship plaster the shoreline. In taking the island the Americans ground forces suffered their heaviest casualties of the Pacific war, including 7,500 dead. Over 5,000 US Navy personnel died in kamikaze suicide attacks on their ships, 38 of which were sunk.

THE DESTRUCTION OF JAPAN

FOR SOME time the islands of Japan remained beyond the range of land-based American bombers. But the capture of the Mariana Islands in June-August 1944 gave the USAAF a springboard from which to launch its B-29 heavy bombers against Japan's cities.

From November 1944 the B-29s of 21st Bomber Command had concentrated on precision attacks on Japanese war industry, achieving only limited success. At the beginning of 1945 the emphasis was switched to a general urban bombing offensive aimed at demoralizing the population and exploiting the particular vulnerability of the close-packed Japanese cities to incendiary raids.

The match was put to the Tokyo tinder box on the night of 9/10 March 1945 when nearly 300 B-29s launched a devastating fire

Below: A Japanese aircraft falls blazing from the sky during the fight for the Marianas in June 1944.

Left: Boeing B-29 Superfortress bombers over Yokohama on 29 May 1945. Introduced to combat in 1944, the B-29 was used exclusively in the Pacific. Its advanced technology included pressurization in the nose and parts of the fuselage and remote-controlled gun turrets. Cruising at 220mph at a height of 30,000ft, the B-29 could carry 5,000 pounds of bombs over a range of 1,600 miles or a maximum payload of 20,000 pounds over short ranges. While the bombers levelled Japan's cities, US submarines tightened the grip on Japan by sinking the shipping on which Japanese war industry depended for its oil and raw materials.

raid which destroyed over 250,000 buildings, killed at least 100,000 people and drove another million into the countryside. Operating with almost complete freedom, 21st Bomber Command levelled city after city. By the end of June, approximately half of the built-up areas of Tokyo, Nagoya, Osaka, Kawasaki, Kobe and Yokohama had been consumed by firestorms. Coastal shipping movements were halted as American bombers sowed thousands of acoustic and magnetic mines in the waters around the Japanese home islands. By the end of July there were virtually no targets left.

Opposite: Carriers and aircraft, the foundation of American air power in the Pacific. Curtiss SB2C Helldiver bombers return to the carrier *Hornet* after a strike against Japanese shipping in the China Sea, January 1945. The powerful Helldiver was a difficult aircraft to fly and never popular with aircrew, who nicknamed it 'Son of a Bitch, Second Class'.

Right: The flight deck of the US carrier *Bunker Hill* after direct hits by two kamikaze aircraft within the space of one minute on 11 May 1945 during the battle for Okinawa.

BUILDING THE A-BOMB

AT DAWN on 16 July 1945 a colossal fireball burst over the New Mexico Desert, fusing the sand to glass and exploding with a force equivalent to 20,000 tons of TNT. A huge mushroom cloud boiled thousands of feet into the sky. With the testing of the first atomic bomb, a new era in warfare had dawned.

After the attack on Pearl Harbor, many of the Allies' most brilliant scientific brains were gathered together in a specially built laboratory complex at Los Alamos in New Mexico. By 1945 about 125,000 people were engaged on the top-secret Manhattan Project to build an atomic bomb. It was only after the war that Allied scientific teams investigating Germany's atomic weapons programme discovered that German research into nuclear weapons lagged behind the Allies by at least two years. Hitler's bomb remained a fantasy.

Only in America could the massive resources necessary to develop the bomb be concentrated. The eventual cost was some two billion dollars. Three weeks after the desert test, the bomb was used against Japan. President Roosevelt's successor, Harry S. Truman, had been advised that an invasion of mainland Japan would cost up to a million casualties. To bring a speedy end to the war in the Pacific, and to provide a demonstration of US military power to the Soviet Union, Truman sanctioned the use of the bomb against Japanese cities.

On 6 August an American B-29 heavy bomber dropped a Uranium-235 version of the bomb, the torpedo-shaped 'Little Boy' on the city of Hiroshima, killing 78,000 people. On 9 August another B-29 dropped 'Fat Man', a bulbous plutonium bomb, on Nagasaki, where 35,000 died. Japan formally surrendered to the Allies on 2 September.

Opposite: The man who delivered the bomb, Colonel Paul Tibbets, the leader of Crew 15, whose men trained to drop the atomic bombs on Japan. On 6 August 1945 he piloted his B-29, named 'Enola Gay' after his mother, to Hiroshima, releasing the six-ton 'Little Boy' nuclear device from a height of 31,600 feet. The destructive power of the bomb was equal to the bombload of nearly 2,000 B-29s carrying conventional high-explosive.

Opposite: Ground zero. The ruins of Hiroshima a few days after the A-bomb attack. Over 100,000 Japanese were killed by the bombs dropped on Hiroshima and Nagasaki. Later, thousands more died of radiation sickness.

Above Left: A victim of the atomic bomb in a makeshift hospital in Hiroshima. The scars of the city of Hiroshima may now have healed but not the physical scars suffered by survivors who were exposed to the full blast of the bomb.

Above: A mushroom cloud rises to 20,000 feet over Nagasaki after the explosion of the second atomic bomb on 9 August 1945.

AFTERMATH

IN THE late summer of 1945 the world was exhausted by war. The cities of Germany and Japan had been levelled by Allied bombers. In Japan, Hiroshima and Nagasaki had been destroyed by atomic bombs.

Huge areas of Europe and Southeast Asia had been devastated by the fighting. Road, rail and canal systems had been destroyed. Ports were choked with wreckage. In Europe a severe drought followed by a disastrous harvest threatened famine in the worst-hit areas. In the western Soviet Union 25 million people were homeless.

In Europe the future looked bleak. The wartime alliance between the United States, Britain and the Soviet Union was fast breaking up. Europe was being divided into two separate and hostile camps: one in Eastern Europe already dominated by the Soviet Union, the other in Western Europe soon to be rescued from political and economic collapse by the United States. The forward flash point of a new conflict, the Cold War, was a divided Germany and its former capital, Berlin, lying deep in the Soviet zone of occupation.

Below: Captured Nazi standards are tossed on to a pile outside Lenin's tomb in Moscow's Red Square.

The European nations which had gone to war in 1939 did not dictate the terms of peace. The Allied strategic aims of the later war years, and the shape of the postwar world, were determined at the great wartime conference by two non-European powers, the United States and the Soviet Union. Soviet hegemony was established in Eastern Europe. In 1945 Poland, the country for which the British and French had gone to war in 1939, exchanged occupation by the Nazis for a long Soviet tyranny.

Left: Bread is distributed to Berliners in the Russian zone of occupation. In the summer of 1945 economic life in Germany had come to halt. In the cities people searched the rubble for anything they could use or sell. Strict Alllied control of the money supply encouraged a flourishing black market in which cigarettes became the basic unit of exchange. They provided entry to a world of barter in which an antique Persian rug might be exchanged for a sack of potatoes. The black market kept thousands of people on the move, travelling in packed trains in search of scarce items of exchange.

In the Pacific the defeat of Japan ensured American domination of the region. The humiliation which the Japanese had inflicted on the colonial powers in the Far East in 1941-2 meant that the empires which the latter had shed so much blood and treasure to regain would soon be threatened by a tide of nationalism.

Below: The defendants in the dock at the war crimes trial which began in Nuremberg in November 1945. On the left is the bulky figure of Hermann Göring. next to him, with arms folded, is Rudolf Hess, Hitler's former deputy, who was ignored by his co-defendants throughout the trial. On Hess' left are Ribbentrop, formerly the German foreign minister and Field Marshal Keitel, chief of staff of the German Army.

Above: Bleak winter. German refugees from Russian-occupied Eastern Europe on the outskirts of Berlin. In December 1945 one in every five inhabitants of the Western zones of occupation was a refugee, known as a 'displaced person' or DP.

COUNTING THE COST

IT IS estimated that some 64 million people died as a result of the Second World War, 24 million soldiers and 40 million civilians. The Soviet Union suffered the most grievous losses, with 8.6 million soldiers dead or missing and nearly 8 million civilians killed. Recent figures which have emerged from Russian archives suggest this figure may have to be revised upwards. Most of the Soviet civilians, the majority of them Ukrainians and White Russians, died as a result of deprivation, reprisal and forced labour. In relative terms, Poland suffered the worst of all the combatant countries. About eight million people – one in four of the population – had died. The death toll in the Polish capital, Warsaw, was higher than the combined wartime casualties of Britain and the United States.

In Yugoslavia civil and guerrilla war killed at least a million. The number of casualties, military and civilian, in Eastern Europe was swollen by the ferocity of the war waged in this theatre and the German racial oppression of Jews and Slavs. Nevertheless, casualties were bad enough in France, Italy and the Netherlands. Before June 1940 and after November 1942 the French army lost 200,000 dead; 400,000 French civilians died in air raids or concentration camps. Italian losses were 330,000, half of them civilians. In Holland 200,000 – all but 10,000 of them civilians – died as a result of bombing or deportation. Their oppressor, Germany, lost 3.5 million military personnel dead or missing and 2 million civilians. The Western Allies did not suffer such horrific losses, but the price of victory was high. The British armed forces lost 244,000 men and their Commonwealth and imperial allies another 100,000. Some 60,000 British civilians died as a result of bombing by the Luftwaffe and the V-weapons. In the United States there were no civilian casualties of war. American military losses were 292,000 dead or missing. In contrast, the Japanese lost 1.2 million men in battle. Nearly a million Japanese civilians died in the war.

Below: Allied casualties after the abortive cross-channel Dieppe raid of 19 August 1942. The operation, codenamed Jubilee, was intended to soothe Soviet anxiety about the lack of a 'second front' in Europe, but resulted in heavy loss of life. Although the raid remains controversial, it provided Allied planners with much information which was put to good use in the preparation and execution of the Normandy landings in June 1944.